POKER NIGHT

♠

Also by John Vorhaus

POKER NIGHT

WINNING
AT HOME,
AT THE
CASINO,
AND
BEYOND

JOHN VORHAUS

St. Martin's Griffin

New York

www.stmartins.com

Library of Congress Cataloging-in-Publication Data

Vorhaus, John.
    Poker night : winning at home, at the casino, and beyond /
John Vorhaus.—1st ed.
        p.   cm.
    ISBN 0-312-33492-3
    EAN 978-0312-33492-5
    1. Poker.   I. Title.

GV1251.V664   2004
795.4'12—dc22   2004048062

10   9   8   7   6   5   4   3   2

To my parents, who taught me
what beats what

♠

CONTENTS

♠

ACKNOWLEDGMENTS

♠

"Changing agents," a writer once said, "is like changing deck chairs on the *Titanic*. Yet we live in hope." Living in hope these past twenty years, I've changed deck chairs many times and have found only two agents who were ever worth a tin nickel. One, Steve Jacobson, became my lifelong friend and earned my undying gratitude by inviting me into his home game. The other, Greg Dinkin, has guided my poker writing career and constantly astounds me as someone who can actually sell a damn book. Thanks to Greg, I may never change deck chairs on the *Titanic* again.

Every time I write a book I'm off down some rabbit hole of obsessive investigation, which leaves my lovely and long-suffering wife, Maxx Duffy, standing around scratching her head and wondering, *Now, where did that boy get off to?* For all the nights I spent playing in various home games—in the name of research, for Pete's sake!—I thank her for her patience and understanding.

Thanks also to Marian Lizzi at St. Martin's Press for her enthusiasm, optimism, and support. As from Bogie to Claude Rains, "I think this is the beginning of a beautiful friendship."

When I told the boys in my home game about *Poker Night*, naturally there were questions. Questions like: "Will we get free copies?" "What about royalties?" "Are you going to mention *smokehouse*?" and "*You're* writing a poker book? Don't they know you suck?" That's what I love about these guys. They're always there for me, supporting me, encouraging me, and threatening to sue if I use their names. Well, let me spell it out, guys. Yes to free copies, no to royalties, definitely yes to *smokehouse*, and you only *think* I suck. As to the threat of lawsuits, what can I say? Steve, Pete, Ace, Ted, George, Sandy, Craig, Tony, I couldn't have done it without you. If you want to sue, *bring it on!*

FOREWORD

♠

When you've played home poker for thirty-seven years and counting as I have, you've pretty much seen it all. Like the tightwad who
could lose a grand without blinking, but just try asking for ten
bucks from the cold-cut rake and watch him have a meltdown. Or
the diva who claimed she'd never played the game before but
somehow managed to exit stage with everyone's cash.

When I started playing home poker, there was nowhere I could
turn for information—and I incurred many expensive lessons. Had
I read this book *before* I started playing, not only would I have
saved a lot of money, but I also would have been spared a lot of
headaches. From knowing which chips to use to establishing rules
to teaching strategy, everything you need to start a home poker
game and *win* in a home poker game is in this book.

When I read the book that you're now holding, I realized that
when it comes to home poker, we're all in this together. We love
the game. We love it with a passion that nonplayers have trouble

comprehending. As Vorhaus puts it in these pages, we know what it means to put the game first, and we know why that's good.

We love to win. Whether we're playing against our boss, our brother-in-law, our own sweet wife, we play for keeps. And we love the game. We love the chance to get together in a place where the normal rules of order don't apply. What a pleasure that is in these tightly controlled lives we lead!

Poker Night tells you everything you need to know to host a successful home poker game. From where to find players for your game, to what to give them to eat, to how to relieve them of their cash, you'll find it all here.

And not just home poker, either, because there's plenty of strategy here to get you going in casino poker or on the internet. I'm not saying it'll happen for sure, but it might just be that this book starts you down the road that leads to a seat in the spotlight at a big televised tournament where I'll be critiquing your play. Stranger things have happened.

But you know what? If that never happens, it really doesn't matter, because all by itself, home poker is really something special. If you don't know that already, you will by the time you've finished reading this book. You'll have some laughs and you'll improve your game. You'll probably even lower your blood pressure if you follow the advice in the upcoming pages!

Poker Night will tell you what to look for in a home poker game, and then how to beat every game you find. Plus it's a fun, great read. So read the book. Play the game. And whatever you do, don't forget: Never try to bluff a sucker.

—Vince Van Patten,
television host of *The World Poker Tour*

INTRODUCTION

♠

I've been playing poker since I was a child old enough to hold cards and chips in my pudgy little hands. Like so many of us, I played first with my family, hunched over the kitchen table and crowing with triumph at a profit of pennies. Later, I expanded my poker horizons to friends and schoolmates, and explored the bizarre outer limits of wildcard games—night baseball, Dr Pepper, and the legendary and long-forgotten one-up, two-up, high-low strawberry. I once pissed off my sister because her boyfriend was more interested in playing poker with me than going out with her. My college games were all-night dormstorms of vodka bombs and tequila braindeaths; sunrise always seemed to take us by surprise. When I became a wage-earning adult, home poker became a staple of my social life, and the monthly game in which I now play has gone on uninterrupted for more than twenty years.

I've played poker all over the world: on makeshift tables of stacked backpacks in youth hostels; on Caribbean beaches with the cards held down by stones to keep them from blowing away;

in places where the game is illegal, and "Joe sent me" countersigns are required. I'm an honorary member of the *Pokerlaget*, a ladies-only home poker society in Norway, where money never changes hands, but the fight is fierce as a bear pit. I'm wearing my *Poker-laget* sweatshirt—damn proudly, I might add—even as I write these words.

One of the defining moments of my life came not at a poker game but en route to one, elsewhere in Scandinavia. I had taken the subway to a certain strange neighborhood in Stockholm and found myself standing on a street corner with a map in one hand, a scrawled address in the other, street signs in Swedish all around me, and no clue in my head about which way to turn. I was lost, but giddy. And why? Because by accident or design, I had put myself in the position of having to make a tricky decision based on incomplete information. I was, in other words, solving a puzzle. And that, I suddenly realized, is the essence of poker: making tricky decisions based on incomplete information. No wonder I love the game.

In this book I hope and plan to share that love, or perhaps just reinforce the gene you carry already. I'll show you how to host a game, and tell you what you need to turn your house into a home poker paradise. I'll teach you the various variations of poker: the popular and obscure ones, and the ones they play on TV. We'll talk about recruiting players, establishing house rules, and setting betting limits so that everyone's playing for meaningful amounts, but no one's getting hurt too bad.

And then, when all that's done, I'll show you how to beat the living crap out of everyone you play!

It's a nice dichotomy, so let's dwell on it for a second. On one hand, for the sake of starting and sustaining a healthy home poker game, you need to be a gracious and thoughtful host. On the other hand, for the sake of winning beer money and bragging rights, you need to be a rapacious predator. This book will teach you how to do both; how, in fact, to appear to be a lovable loser while secretly exploiting and manipulating your opponents to the benefit of your bankroll.

Maybe you don't like this idea. Maybe you think that poker should be a fun game, purely a social event staged for camaraderie, laughs, and a good time. If that's the case, you can skip the tactical sections of this book, and more power to you. But before you dismiss winning as a goal, I would ask you to consider your own motives. Why don't you want to win? Do you think that it's rude, in some sense, to best your friends in honest competition? Some people do, and home poker is not the game for them. They do very well in cardrooms and casinos, playing against strangers, but when it comes to going *mano a mano* against their coworkers or lodge buddies . . . no, that's something they don't like.

There's a deeper reason, though, for not striving for excellence in poker, or in anything, and it has to do with how we view ourselves and our endeavors in this world. Many of us recognize that *not trying* is a reasonable excuse for *not succeeding*. That is, if we don't give something our best effort, we can always point to that fact as the basis for poor results. If, on the other hand, we give poker (or anything) everything we've got and *still* don't win, well, that's a fairly bitter pill to swallow. So we cloak our fear of failure in indifference toward victory. We're just here for fun, we say, and we let it go at that.

I don't buy it. I don't buy this defeatist attitude, not in poker and not in life. To bastardize Tennyson, 'tis better to have tried and failed than never to have tried at all. I don't want to make this sound bigger than it is—okay maybe I do: Excellence in poker translates into excellence elsewhere. If you take the time and spend the energy to master a thing like poker, you gain the confidence and know-how to master more important things as well.

So. Will home poker change your life? Make you an astronaut? Win you the love of millions (or even one)? Buy you into the World Series of Poker? I wish I could promise all that, for it would certainly help my book sales, and maybe buy *me* into the World Series of Poker, but we all know the truth. Poker is just a game, and home poker is just a game you play at home. It can add real value to your life: provide you a healthy outlet for competitive urges; create a space where the typical rules and taboos of society don't apply; let you play bully for once; help you bond with your buddies; prepare you for casino or online play, and potentially bigger money earnings; and put some bucks in your pocket as well. But it won't whiten your teeth or fix the transmission on your car. It's only a game, after all.

What poker does best is let you forget. A poker game—a good one, anyhow—is so engaging and compelling that while you're playing in it, the everyday worries of your world melt away. You don't *care* if your teeth aren't white. You don't *care* if your car goes *clunk* when you shift. For as long as the game lasts, you're ensorcelled by the puzzle, by the task of making tricky decisions based on incomplete information. You're completely and utterly in the moment, and is this not what meditation seeks to achieve? No past, no future, only the perfect now. This, I believe, is why so many of us guard so jealously our time at the table, and give our weekly or monthly home poker games precedence over everything short of (and, in fact, not always entirely short of) weddings, births, and funerals. It's a respite, recess, a chance to say "Time out" to our lives.

Home poker games come in all shapes and sizes. Some moguls

put wads of cash on the table big enough to buy boats. In other games, the players literally haul out piggy banks to fund their play. Some games are men-only, some are women-only, and some don't care about such politically incorrect considerations. In some games, smoking is prohibited (or mandatory). In some games, drinking is prohibited (or mandatory). Some hosts serve lavish buffets, while from others you're lucky to score cold pizza and flat soda. Though home poker is, by definition, not public poker, you don't necessarily find home poker games at home. Social clubs, offices after hours, hotel rooms, apartment complex rec. rooms, even church basements can all house rousing games of pasteboard madness. A good home poker game—and by good I mean a healthy and thriving and reliably ongoing game—is an organic, dynamic, flexible thing. It responds to the needs of the players. If the stakes are so high that no one can afford to lose even once, then the stakes come down. If once a week is too frequent to field a quorum, the schedule gets stretched. If Friday nights don't work, you shift to Tuesday. And so on.

I guess you're reading this book with at least one of several different ideas in mind. You may want to know what it takes to set up and run a poker night. Perhaps you'd like to know the rules and mechanisms of the poker variations typically played in home games. Maybe you're looking for home poker strategy, which, believe me, is far different from cardroom or online poker strategy. Maybe you've been watching poker on television and decided to try your hand. Maybe you're looking for a springboard into the world of public poker. Maybe you don't even know what you're looking for; maybe you got this book as a gift (from, for instance, a spouse who's gently suggesting that you need to get out a little more). Whatever you're looking for, I hope you find it here, and if you don't find it here, I hope you'll take a moment to query me directly. You'll find my e-mail address at my website, *www.vorza.com*, and I welcome your questions on all things having to do with home poker. If I don't know the answer, I'll happily invent one. How does that sound?

If you think I'm being flip, really I'm not. Sometimes the best answer is one you make up on the spot, and deliver with the courage of your convictions. In poker we call this *bluffing*, and it's a skill that's called upon not just in the play of the game, but in running the game as well. What would you do, for instance, if one of your home game players suddenly found that he had an extra card in his hand? Would you pronounce that player's hand dead or declare a misdeal and start over? Either decision could be correct, and either opinion will likely be accepted by the players in your game, so long as you voice it with authority. The controlling idea, then, in running a home poker game, as in so many facets of human interaction, is, *If you can't be right, be loud; if you're loud enough long enough, you will appear to be right.*

I'm not saying you should be a poker night despot. I'm all for consensus, democracy, due process. In a well-wrought home poker game, the players get together and agree on the rules in advance. That said, situations arise that simply are not covered by the rules. In those situations, it's incumbent on someone to step up and *make the call*. Why should you be the one? Because you've read this book, and I've told you it's your job. Uneasy lies the head that wears a crown.

You may have noticed that here in this introduction, in the space of these few pages, I have already proposed a couple of strongly proactive stances. I have encouraged you to *play to win*, and I have counseled you to *run the show*. I want to move you off your diffidence and into a strong, vigorous mind-set because I think you'll get much more out of the game—more enjoyment, more satisfaction, and yes, more money—if you go at it hard. "Proactive poker is winning poker," I always say. "Go big or go home." Well, when you play home poker you're already home, or in someone else's home, or perhaps their converted garage, but wherever you find yourself, I encourage you to take this idea on board. Among other things, it's a permission—a permission we don't often get in life—to go all out and let the chips, literally, fall where they may. I have said that poker gives you the rare opportunity to play bully, and it's one of the things I relish about the game. I've also suggested that a poker game is a place where norms of behavior don't apply: You can do things in a poker game that you'd never get away with in polite society. I'm not saying that you must be ruthless, cunning, and cutthroat to enjoy your home poker game—people take their pleasure in all sorts of different ways—I'm just saying it might do you some good.

In these *Title IX* times, no book of this sort would be complete without the following disclaimer: Though I use mainly male labels throughout—*he* raises, you raise *him* back—please take it as read that I'm referring to men and women alike. Men, after all, hold no monopoly on all things ruthless, cunning, and cutthroat, but until someone comes up with practical gender-neutral third-person pronouns, we'll have to settle for the ones we have.

For many players, social poker is all they need. They're happy with their home game and they neither aspire nor desire to do their thing in public. Others hope that home poker will help them make the transition into the cardrooms of this land or the virtual cardrooms of the internet. For those who plan to take that step, I intend this book to be your map and guide. Between the first page and the last, I propose to take you from where you are—even if where you are is a standing start—to the point where you have enough poker *nous* (a lovely Australian word meaning "knowl-edge" or "sense") to walk into a casino or log onto a poker website, confident that you've got a clue. That's the start of a whole other journey, and there are other books (including some of mine) that can help you walk that road. You'll find them listed in the Recommended Reading section in the back of the book. For now, though, let's just get the cards in the air.

1

WHAT BEATS WHAT?

♠

We learn it by rote. *High card*. We can quote it by heart. *One pair*. Our first significant strategic information. *Two pair*. We feel smug in our certain knowledge. *Trips*. Superior to neophytes who know it not. *Straight*. We teach it to our children. *Flush*. We draw to big hands. *Full house*. We lose to bigger hands. *Four of a kind*. We gawk at monsters. *Straight flush*. We dream our dreams. *Royal flush*.

What beats what: It's the poetry of poker; it's where the game begins.

Funny thing about *what beats what*. People who have no knowledge of poker, people who have literally never played a hand in their lives, can nevertheless tell you the ranks of hands. They don't know how they know, they just know. They can't tell you their anniversary, or what they had for breakfast, but they're sure to the core of their being that a flush beats a straight, and aces are the highest pair there is.

For those who don't know, here's *what beats what* in simple chart form. You can photocopy it and have it handy for your less-poker-literate friends. Yes, it's a crutch, but one that some find useful, at least while they're learning the game.

The Ranks of Hands in Poker

Type of hand	Example
High card	A♣-Q♥-T♥-4♠-3♦
One pair	K♥-K♦-J♠-9♥-2♣
Two pair	7♥-7♠-6♣-6♥-Q♦
Three of a kind	T♥-T♦-T♠-9♥-5♣
Straight	T♣-9♥-8♣-7♠-6♦
Flush	A♥-J♥-T♥-3♥-2♥
Full House	9♣-9♦-9♠-2♠-2♣
Four of a kind	5♥-5♣-5♦-5♠-K♦
Straight flush	5♦-4♦-3♦-2♦-A♦
Royal flush	A♠-K♠-Q♠-J♠-T♠

If two players have the same sort of hand, the winner is determined by the top card or cards. Your ace-high flush beats my king-high flush, but my ten-high straight beats your eight-high straight, but your three sixes beat my three threes, and so on. Should our hands be identical at the top, we keep going down until they diverge. Two pair of aces and kings, for example, beats two pair of aces and queens.

The relative strength of a poker hand is based on its rarity. The less likely you are to make a hand, the higher it sits in the pantheon of *what beats what*. In a standard five-card poker holding, for example, you'll start with two pair once every twenty hands or so, but you'll go more than 4,100 hands, on average, before picking up a pat four of a kind. (*Pat*, by the way, is poker idiom for "made" or "complete." I'll try to define these terms as I go along, but I won't beat a dead horse about it, any more than I'll dump more statistics and numbers on you than I have to. In any case, you'll find a glossary around here somewhere.)

The simplest way to gauge your chances of winning with any poker hand is to think of each hand as a horse race. Good cards equal a big head start, and if you have a big head start, you're more likely to finish first. If you always yield the head start to the other guy, you'll come up short more often than not. Suppose you hold a hand like this:

In a typical game of draw poker, you'll discard the deuce and draw one card, trying to hit a nine to complete your inside straight. With four nines and forty-three not-nines remaining in the deck, your chances of plucking that precious nine are roughly one in eleven. That is, for every eleven times you try, ten times you'll fail, and ten times you'll lose your bet. Your wily foe, meanwhile, started out with this hand:

He might draw three cards to his pair of aces, but with his big head start—a pair of aces against your possible straight—he'll win your money ten times out of eleven, *whether he improves his hand or not!* That's why momma always told you not to draw to an inside straight. We'll explore this concept in greater detail later, but for now just recognize the difference between an optimist and a realist in poker: The optimist has high hopes; the realist has the cash. To be the one with the cash, simply refuse to bet unless you're ahead.

There are times, of course, when it makes sense to play a hand that's temporarily in second place. Consider this example.

You hold:

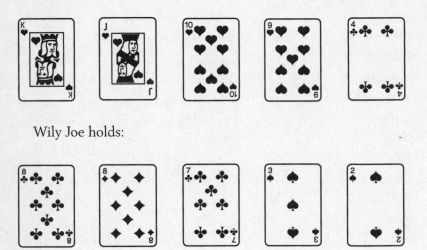

Wily Joe holds:

He has a better hand than you right now, but with any king, jack, ten, or nine giving you a higher pair, any queen giving you a straight, and any heart giving you a flush, if you throw away your four of clubs and draw one card, you'll improve to a better hand than his slightly more than half the time. Naturally there are times when he will improve too, but let's let that go for now. Thinking of a strong starting hand as a *lead horse* and a good draw-ing hand as a *fast horse*, here's your first winning concept in poker:

Rule Book

Be the *lead horse,* or be a *fast horse.* Always try to play only when the odds are in your favor.

And that's a beautiful thing about poker: If the odds aren't in your favor, *you don't have to play!* Every time you're dealt a hand, you have the option to fold . . . just throw it away. While aggressiveness—*Go big or go home*—is certainly a winning component of poker, don't forget the "go home" part of the equation. Every hand is a horse race. If you don't like your chances in this race, just scratch yourself. There'll be another race along in a minute.

Now I'm going to tell you a secret about many home poker players: *They hate to fold!* They may have been thinking about and dreaming about this poker night for days or weeks, and now that it's finally here, the last thing they want to do is sit on the sidelines and watch the action go by. In my home game, we call this the Pacoima Syndrome, as in, "I didn't drive all the way from Pacoima to fold." So they'll forget the horse race. They'll forget the unfavorable odds. They'll draw to those inside straights, because the alternative, for many of them, is too horrible to contemplate. Can you see the huge advantage this gives you? Sure, they'll get lucky from time to time—hit that unlikely inside straight—but in the long run the odds even out, and the player who insists on having the head start will definitely come out ahead.

♦ ♦ ♦ Low Poker Values

I don't want to burden you with too much *what beats what* all at once, but you need to know (if you do not know already) that poker is often played with the low hand winning instead of the high hand, or with the best high hand and the best low hand splitting the pot. High-low games are *action* games, ones that encourage lots of betting and build big pots. Because every hand offers the possibility of two winners, players tend to stick around—especially those who didn't drive all the way from Pacoima to fold! For we who play to win, this makes our "have the head start" strategy that much more correct.

There is some argument in home game circles as to what the best possible low hand is. Some say it's 5-4-3-2-A. Others say it's 6-5-4-3-2 because how could an ace, the highest card in the deck, be low? Still others argue that 6-5-4-3-2 *can't* be a low because it's a straight, and a straight is a higher hand than trips, two pair, and so on. Without hoping to settle the argument forever (the matter, after all, is one of opinion) let me just say that in most home games, and virtually any cardroom where low or high-low poker is played, the best possible low is the so-called *wheel* or *bicycle*, 5-4-3-2-A. Yes, I know it's a straight, but, by tradition and convention, the straight doesn't negate the low, nor, for that matter, does a flush. Yes, I know there's an ace, but in this case the ace does duty as a low card—the lowest card in the deck.

The value of a low hand is measured from the top down. That is, a 5-4-3-2-A low is better than a 6-4-3-2-A low because the top card in the first instance, the five, is lower than the top card in the second instance, the six. If the top cards are the same, the second-highest card is considered, and so on. When I happen to have 6-5-4-3-2 and you have 6-4-3-2-A, you win, because your second-highest card, the four, is lower than my second-highest card, the five. Let's chart it out:

The Ranks of Low Hands in Poker

5-4-3-2-A (best)

6-4-3-2-A

6-5-3-2-A

7-6-5-3-A

7-6-5-3-2

and so on

As I said, there's more than one opinion on whether *wheel low equals best low.* In many home games, the best possible low is 6-4-3-2-A, and a wheel, while pretty, is a straight and a loser for low. At the end of the day, you and your friends will decide which way to play your lows, but if you're looking for authority, here, I'll lend you mine: "*Poker Night* says that wheel low is best low, so that's the way we'll play it here." Again, it doesn't matter which way you go, so long as you're consistent and clear. The last thing you want is a big dispute at the *showdown* (when cards are revealed and winners determined) over which lows are valid, and which is best. The best way to avoid these disputes is to agree on such things in advance. When everyone has been made aware that wheels play for low, they have no one to blame but themselves if they fail to recognize or remember that fact.

If you have no experience playing poker, no personal knowledge of the ol' *what beats what*, do yourself the favor of grabbing a deck of cards right now and dealing yourself a few dozen five-card hands. You'll quickly get a sense of which hands you see frequently (hands with one or two pair; hands with three or four low cards) and which hands are much more rare (straights, flushes, and five-card lows). This sense (called *card sense*) will be your principal analytical tool when you set out to measure the strength of your hand, and your chances of winning the pot, against the strength of your opponents' holdings. If you're better at gauging their strength than they are at gauging yours, you'll be a winner in poker. Why? Because in poker—hold on to your hat, now—*luck doesn't matter at all!*

I'm not saying luck doesn't exist. Of course it exists. If there's one card left in the deck that you need to make your hand, and you catch it, baby, that's lucky. You've hit a long shot, and that won't happen very often for you. But guess what? It won't happen any more often, nor any less often, for me. You may outdraw me this time, and I may outdraw you next time, but who cares? *Luck evens out in the end*. Many players don't believe this. They see themselves as luckier or unluckier than average, but they're wrong. The fact is that players create their own luck (or what seems to be luck), based on the decisions they make. As it happens, there are sound strategic reasons for persuading your opponents that you're a lucky player, as opposed to a talented one or a skilled one, but don't ever fall for your own PR. Everyone is exactly as lucky as everyone else.

Don't believe me? Let's flip some coins. I happen to have a sack of Sacagawea dollars right here. I'm flipping one now. Call it in the air. Did you call heads? Sorry, it was tails. I win a dollar. Let's try again. Heads? Nope, sorry, tails again. Now you owe me two dollars. Looks like you're 100 percent unlucky. Okay, third trial. You call tails . . . and it's tails! You win! You're back to a dollar in debt, and now only 67 percent unlucky. Let's flip again. In fact, let's flip again another two or three million times and hey, look at that: About half the time, the coin lands heads and the other half the coin lands tails.

But this is kiddie math, right? You know that a coin flip is a fifty-fifty proposition. Always has been, always will be. Okay, but what if a fifty-fifty proposition didn't have a fifty-fifty payout? What if I paid you $1.10 every time you won, and you paid me only $.90 every time you lost? You could make some money on that margin, couldn't you? Given enough time and enough trials, you'll win a buttload of Sacagawea dollars—every last one in my sack. Why? It's not that you're lucky. It's that you're winning more than your share when you win and losing less than your share when you lose. This is called *betting with the best of it*, and it's the heart and soul of successful poker.

Now, you may be thinking, and I wouldn't blame you if you were, that this is a silly example. What kind of moron would tolerate such tilted odds on an even money proposition? No kind of moron would, of course, *if he knows the odds*. When it's a coin flip, it's easy to see the odds. Poker situations are more complex, but the numbers don't matter nearly so much as the concept of betting with the best of it. Suppose we're playing low draw poker, also known as *lowball*. I hold:

You hold:

For the sake of this example, we'll assume that we're going to bet even money and both draw one card. My draw looks pretty good. If I catch a three, I've got a perfect wheel, the best possible low. At first glance, you seem to have the same draw. If you catch a four, you've got a perfect wheel too, and we tie. But what if we both draw sixes? You win. What if we both draw sevens? You win. Eights? Nines? Tens? Any time we both hit the same card, *you win*. We're betting even money, but you have a huge advantage, because *you win all ties!*

Most of your opponents wouldn't think about this. Even if they could see your cards and knew they had the worst of it, they'd still look at their own beautiful four-card low and say, "Man, I'm going for it!" Let 'em go for it. Let 'em go for it till the cows come home. Every time they make a wrong decision, you're making money, whether they happen to get lucky this time or not. In fact, getting lucky this time is one of the worst things that can happen to them, because then they'll start to believe in luck, and they'll take even worse draws with even worse odds next time around. This is why I say that players create their own luck based on the decisions they make. If you make better decisions than your opponents—decisions based on information and simple analysis, as opposed to superstition and blind faith—you're bound to beat them in the end, no matter what specific outcome comes this time.

Now you know *what beats what*. It's not the cards. It's the play-ers who hold them. If you stick to the principle of betting with the best of it, you'll generally beat the game. It's really as simple as that.

Before we get around to beating the game, though, we first have to *spread* (set up) the game, so let's turn our attention next to that.

2

THE GULP LIMIT

♠

No one has to play home poker, you know. If you live in California, New Jersey, or some twenty other states in the union (or Canada, Australia, Estonia, and many other civilized countries), you're probably within shouting distance of a perfectly safe, perfectly legal public cardroom. Thanks to the internet, you can play online poker against real opponents for real money, in the nude if you like, any time you like. And planes fly to Las Vegas every day. So then there's the question "Why?" Why play home poker at all? I can think of a few reasons.

First, it's fun. Social poker played among friends, colleagues, or peers is just a flat-out pleasant way to spend an afternoon or evening—or afternoon, evening, night, next morning, and next afternoon. Jokes get told. Smack gets talked. Bragging rights get won. People have the feeling of participating in something, being part of an event, in a way that cocktail parties or dinners out just can't match. Further, many home poker games are safe havens, either of gender where boys can be boys or girls can be girls, or just of being, places where, unlike an office, school, or church or synagogue of your choice, you can let your hair down (even if, like me, you have none).

Second, it's a training ground. If you've never played poker in a casino, or find the idea of playing against unseen internet opponents to be frightening or bizarre, your home poker game is a controlled environment of known opponents where you can take your time learning the rhythms of the game and honing your strategic skills. To be honest, cardrooms aren't nearly as daunting as public poker newbies imagine them to be—not everyone you meet is named Doc or Ace or wears a World Series of Poker championship bracelet—but this is a case where perception is reality. If you feel intimidated, you'll *be* intimidated. Home poker lets you get your feet wet, and home poker plus the advice in this book will give you a good tactical and psychological grounding for the day you decide to step up to public play, either in cardrooms or online.

Third, it's a buzz. Let's not overlook this point. Gambling—wagering on outcomes—is a very powerful stimulant. The first time you find yourself contesting a big pot and investing all your hope for happiness on the turn of the next card, believe me, you will *feel* it. Your fingers will tingle and your palms will sweat. You'll get the coppery taste of adrenaline in your mouth. Your pulse will race and your temples will throb. Your heart will feel like it wants to explode through your chest like some slimy space alien exploding out of a host body. Good times!

Then there's the money. In a raked game, such as you'll find in most cardrooms, the house takes a percentage of each pot, so every player who wants to win has to overcome not just his foes but also the house's cut. It's easier to make a profit at home because you need only beat your opponents, not your opponents *and* the house. Not only that, the quality of your foes at home will likely be lower than in the general poker population, making them generally easier to best.

Once real money starts changing hands, the following question always arises: "Is this legal?" Well, with so many state and local jurisdictions to consider, I can't tell you for sure that home poker is strictly legal where you are. In many places, so-called "social gaming" is legal so long as the house isn't dealing itself a built-in edge (by banking a blackjack game, for example) or raking the pot for profit. In practical terms, home poker is almost universally ignored by the forces of law because, hey, why bother? I'm no lawyer, and I certainly won't post your bail if you're busted, but I think that on the list of things you need to worry about, getting arrested at a social poker game is somewhere between getting hit by an asteroid and having nothing to wear when the Queen invites you to tea. Nevertheless, I know of at least one person who said he'd never play home poker because: "I might want to run for office someday." Well, if it's your trip, take it.

Having decided to host a home poker game, your first order of business is filling the seats. Five players is the realistic minimum number for a playable game. Six is better, seven or eight is best. To find these worthies, simply spread the word among friends, coworkers, golf cronies, fellow inmates, whatever. Set a date far enough in advance that people can put it firmly on their calendars, then keep recruiting till your table is full. Don't be surprised to find enthusiastic responses from unexpected quarters. Since poker has come out of the back room in recent years and has shed its tawdry image in television's bright lights, the game is attracting interest from people who would not formerly have given it a second thought. I'm not saying that your priest, rabbi, minister, mother-in-law, or town councilor will take a seat in your game, but . . . okay, maybe they will.

As it has for so many other group activities, the modern miracle of e-mail has made establishing and organizing a sign-up list a snap. With surprisingly little effort, you can grow your list to the point where filling the game is merely a matter of setting a date, sending the word, and locking up seats on a first-come, first-served basis. Thanks further to the internet, you can hunt up other home game players in your hometown, either by querying poker discussion groups like *rec.gambling.poker* or posting your name or your game to home game clearinghouses like *www.homepokergames. com*, a nifty little online matchmaking service that, at least as of this writing, does duty as an online link between interested players and the home games in their area.

No matter who your players are or how you find them, there's one thing you'll want them to have and no, it's not loose money, it's *commitment*. Whether you play once a week, once a month, or only at the equinox and solstice, everyone in the game must understand and agree that *on poker night, poker comes first*. Otherwise . . . sad scenario . . . a couple of late scratches, an unexplained absence, some lame excuse about Ebola Virus . . . next thing you know, it's just two or three of you passing each other's money back and forth all night and basically hating your absent friends.

So seek players who will make the game a priority, and—my advice—seek them regardless of gender. Not to challenge the sanctity of the boys' (or girls') club, but why restrict your search for able poker players to half the human gene pool? Enthusiasm, reliability, good sportsmanship, quick wit, ready cash, *commitment* . . . these are the qualities you want in each and every member of your poker gang. Don't worry too much whether they pee lid-up or lid-down. This is the twenty-first century, after all.

Male or female, the first thing they'll want to know is, "What are the stakes?" or, more to the point, "How much do I stand to lose?" Setting stakes can be a tricky business. On one hand, the money has to be meaningful, or no one will take the game seriously, thus neutralizing two of poker's key elements: fortitude and the bluff. Then again, if it costs too much to play, either you won't find willing competitors or people will go broke too fast and the game will fall apart.

To establish the right stakes for your game, first locate your group's *gulp limit*, the amount of money that makes most players in your game go *gulp*, at least just a little. The gulp limit is, of course, a sliding scale. I know games where they battle for pennies with the intensity of rabid javelinas. In other games, people spew *Big Bens* (or *Franklins*—hundred-dollar bills) into play from midnight till dawn without batting an eye. A good way to identify your own gulp limit is to ask this question: "If I misplaced [blank] amount of money, would I feel real regret?" Then start filling in the blank with higher and higher numbers until the answer changes from no to yes. That's your gulp limit.

Gulp limits change over time. Once when I was a kid I lost exactly 65 cents pitching nickels and cried. The first time I played cardroom poker, I won twenty bucks and felt like Donald Trump. These days I routinely buy into poker games for a thousand dollars or more, knowing full well that that grand may be going home as someone else's guest. I don't love to lose—no one does, and no one should—but for the type of poker I play, about a grand is my gulp limit now.

Gulp limits change over time because people improve their play and "step up in class" and also because they get used to gambling and build up a tolerance to the buzz of the bet. The dollar wager that caused an adrenaline frenzy the first time you made it simply doesn't have the same impact a thousand bets later. Because of this, it's a good idea to start your game small, whatever you define small to be, and plan to raise the stakes over time. Remember that you're serving the long-term goal of building and sustaining a healthy and ongoing home poker game. Keeping the stakes small to start gives everyone a chance to learn the game, *love* the game, and build confidence in their ability to compete, plus acclimate to the buzz. Be patient. There'll be plenty of time later to strip-mine everyone's wallets.

Having identified your group's gulp limit, you next need to establish appropriate betting limits. Most poker games establish a minimum and a maximum allowable bet size, and these minimums and maximums are the *limits* for that game. In so-called nickel-dime poker games the limits are, you guessed it, a nickel and a dime. In bigger games, you might have limits of $1 and $2, $5 and $10, $100 and $200, and so on. In the biggest games, such as the ones you see on TV these days, the betting structure is *no limit*, which means that players can wager up to everything they've got on the turn of any card.

At the start of each game, all players will make an initial *buy-in*, or purchase of chips. The buy-in should be roughly twenty-five to thirty times the size of your top limit or *big bet*, for example $100 in a $2–4 limit game. Note that the higher the ratio between the betting limits and buy-in, the more bets a player can make with his initial buy-in, and the more "play" there is said to be in the game. Let's say you've figured out that your guys' gulp limit is about fifty bucks. That's what you set as the buy-in, but now you have to make sure that everyone gets appropriate action for their investment. It would be ludicrous, for example, to set betting limits of $10 and $20, since every player losing his first hand would have to buy more chips. More appropriate limits would be $1 and $2. If you want to give players more play, just drop the limits to $.50 and $1.

Buy-ins and betting limits, though, tell only half the story, because it's reasonable to expect that somewhere along the line someone is going to lose his or her initial buy-in and have to *rebuy*, or buy more chips. Some nights—some *long* nights—players go through several rebuys, and the sum of these rebuys is said to be the *swing* of a game, where swing equals the amount of money a player can expect to win or to lose on an exceptionally good or an exceptionally bad night. Swings of 100 times the big bet are not unheard of in home poker games. While it's not likely that someone will drop $400 in a $2–4 game, it can happen, and if such an outcome would have your poker pals reaching for their razor blades, they probably shouldn't play in a game as big as yours.

In the name of full disclosure, then, tell prospective players in your game what they can expect in terms of three things: betting limit, buy-in, and swing. Tell them, for example, that it's $1–2 limit poker with a $50 buy-in and possible swings of a couple of Big Bens. Armed with this information, they can decide for themselves whether they want to jump in.

3

HOW TO HOST A GAME

♠

Okay, you've set a date, lined up some players, and established the betting limits at anything from nickel and dime to "How much ya got?" Let's turn our attention next to the physical needs of the game. You know: tables, chairs, poker chips, onion dip, absinthe, and smuggled Cuban cigars.

It's not necessary to own a poker table, though it's so cool if you do. My own, a bequest from my father-in-law, is a bleached-oak beauty of some vintage, with a pristine leather top and a custom-made Plexiglas cover. Store-bought poker tables, or even lay-on poker tops, can be pricey, and if there's no money in your household budget for a poker table (because the kids are whining for luxuries like, you know, food), you might try the poor man's poker table, a piece of three-quarter-inch octagon-cut plywood swathed in green felt. Even your dining room table will do in a pinch, provided you cover it with pads or a thick cloth or both. You don't want poker chips dinging the finish, God knows, and you also don't want them careening off the table every time you toss in a bet. Make sure you have plenty of comfortable chairs. This may seem self-evident, but not everyone has seven or eight decent chairs on hand at home, and the poor sucker stuck sitting on the step stool all night may send you his chiropractic bill.

Now to chips. Poker chips are key. Avoid those plinky little wiffle-ridged drugstore plastic jobbies at all cost. Why? You may not believe this, but it's hard to play serious poker with frivolous chips. So much of what makes poker *poker* is the visceral experience of the thing, and cheap chips, well . . . you wouldn't serve cognac in a jelly jar, would you? No, you want clay or clay-composite chips: chips with heft and feel and substance; gravitas. These you can find at any game store or gaming supply house or, inevitably, on the internet. Also try trolling for poker chips at yard sales and flea markets, where you can get a swell set with some history and quality for not much money, if you're prepared to shop around and haggle mercilessly. In all events, you'll want 500 or so chips in three or four different colors to host a full game. Here's a typical color/denomination breakdown for a 500-chip set.

500 Poker Chips

Value	Color	Quantity
$1	White	150
$5	Red	150
$25	Green	100
$100	Black	100

A Couple of Don'ts: First, don't buy chips with dollar denominations because you may, for example, want to use your white chips as $1 chips in one game, but $.50 chips in another, and if the stated value and the assigned value of the chips differ, it tends to confuse some players, especially late in the evening when the level gets low in the absinthe bottle. Second, not to wax conservative or anything, but do yourself a big favor (learn from my painful mistake) and stick to conventional colors. I bought some lavender chips once—what was I thinking?—and they languish in my closet, too embarrassing to be shown the light of day.

If you want to take it to the next level, you can custom-order poker chips in various styles and designs, with your name, initials, or family crest snazzily embossed in gold. Custom chips can get pricey, but they're worth it. A good set of chips will last a lifetime or longer, and the investment amortized over years of play amounts to literally only pennies per game. Take the long view. Buy the most, best chips you can. You'll thank yourself later—and whoever eventually inherits your chips will thank you, too.

(As an aside, you may not have thought of this, but poker chips make a wonderful wedding present. They do last a lifetime, they're not something most young couples buy for themselves, and they beat the heck out of a seventh gravy boat or toaster oven.)

Chips can be old, but cards should be new, for there's nothing worse than playing poker with dog-eared, grubby, or sticky cards, plus . . . where the deuce did that deuce of diamonds go? Plastic cards like those manufactured by Kem can be used forever, and so make another easily amortized investment, especially since they're not that much more expensive than regular cards to start with. You'll want to have two decks on hand, with differently colored backs, so that one can be shuffled, or *made*, while the other deck's in play.

The type and amount of food to provide for a poker game depends to a large degree on when the game is starting. If everyone's coming to the game straight from work, you'll want to have on hand something that looks like dinner. If the game's starting later, and people will have eaten their evening meal already, then you can get by with potato chips, nuts, candy, and cut veggies. Don't overbuy unless you like leftovers. In my experience, poker players are hungry—to play poker.

Though you may be hosting the game, you have no obligation to pay the freight alone. It's typical in home poker that all the players help cover this cost, and the easiest way to do so is to subtract an appropriate amount of money from each player's initial buy-in. This may be $5 or $10 taken from a $100 buy-in, for example, depending, of course, on how lavish the spread and/or how top-shelf the booze.

Talking of booze, should yours be a drinking game? My devious answer is yes—for everyone except you. As John Fox wrote in his immortal *Play Poker, Quit Work and Sleep Till Noon*:

> If you are a **very** bad player to start with, drinking probably won't hurt your game too much. For **anyone** else, one drink is too much, two drinks are ridiculous.

While it's true that most serious poker players don't drink while they play, it's also true that most home games are not, strictly speaking, serious affairs. Nor should they be, for if poker night isn't, at minimum, fun, it's defeating its own purpose. But different people have different ideas of fun. For some of us, fun is taking our friends to the cleaners. For others, fun is knocking back a quart of Old Throatburne while calling every bet. Drinking players tend to be very generous, and if you can get on the receiving end of their largesse, well, you'll probably be happy with the outcome. Just don't let 'em drive.

But this whole approach to food and drink varies widely from game to game and group to group. Just as water finds its level, your game will find its own organic answers to the questions of what, and how much, to eat or drink.

Or smoke.

I know some home games where smoking is barred with an almost religious fervor. In other games, the right to smoke is defended with equal zeal, and the lighting up of stogies is vital to the ritual, part of the point of the game. Hey, I'm the last person on the planet to tell you that you should or shouldn't smoke, but I will say this: In modern America, it's often harder to fill the seats in a smoking game than a nonsmoking one. Also, let's face it, smokers are at a disadvantage in smoke-filled rooms, especially in places like my home state of California, where smoking in public has been virtually banned and you may have encountered your last smoke-filled room sometime in the past century. With this in mind, you might want to level the playing field by declaring your game nonsmoking, but also providing a convenient outdoor area for those who choose to inhale.

If you're hosting the game, you'll also be expected to *bank* the game; that is, swap buy-ins for chips at the start, and cash everyone out at the end. You'll need change—singles if yours is a $1 limit game; coins if you're playing smaller—and you can meet this need simply by buying your food and drink for the game with large bills and taking lots of change in change.

Also, don't forget to have enough cash on hand to cover everyone's winnings. This won't be a problem if you win, but what if you're in the hole—let's say *way* in the hole? There's nothing more frustrating to a player than putting up big numbers in a poker game and having to take a marker for the money he's won. You may all be friends, but this is *poker*, man, and winners expect to get paid. The bank is obligated to have enough cash on hand to cover his own losses (heaven forefend!) as well as everyone else's wins.

Here's a quandary that you'll eventually face if you're the bank: One night, Gatling Gary comes into the game with all guns blazing and soon, through a combination of bad luck and bad play, finds himself down to the felt: broke, busted, tap city. Well, Gary didn't drive all the way from Pacoima just to turn around and go *back* to Pacoima. He wants to play on, on the finger, and he's looking to you to advance him the scratch. Should you extend credit to Gatling Gary? I gotta go with my man Shakespeare on this:

> *Neither a borrower nor a lender be;*
> *For loan oft loses both itself and friend,*
> *And borrowing dulls the edge of husbandry.*

Forgetting for the moment that you may never see the money again, the real problem with "reloading a soldier in the heat of combat" is that it pushes him outside his gulp limit. He may have come in with, say, $200 to commit to the game, but now, having run badly and gone broke, he wants to blast past his preset stop-loss to the tune of three or four or more hundred dollars. We call this phenomenon *hemorrhaging at the wallet*. It's not good for the player—and it's really not good for the game. While you might score a big win over Gary this week, he may be filled with such remorse that he never returns, in which case your game has lost a player. There's something in here about golden geese; metaphorical construction left to the reader.

In the real world, of course, it's not so cut-and-dried. Gary might be your boss or your underling or your brother-in-law, and you may be in no position to deny him his loan, even though you know that everyone will end up ruing it, including you, Gary, and Mrs. Gary, your sister. At times like these, it helps to have house rules to hide behind. If there's a stated rule against extending credit, then you'll have an argument that stands up to the weight of Gary's importunings. "Sorry, Gary man, I'd love to lend you the money, but like the sign says, 'No Credit,' so don't ask."

Now that we're talking about house rules, let's talk about them some more, and see how a vigorous set of house rules can dampen conflict and keep the dolphins of dissent safely out in the sea of tranquillity.

4

HOUSE RULES AND PROCEDURES

♠

Years ago I had a dream. I was heading across the Mojave Desert to Las Vegas in a gold-flake Cadillac Eldorado. A '57, I believe. I wasn't driving. Elvis Presley was. (True fact! Well, true dream fact.) At one point, the King looked over at me and said, "The rules don't confine, they define." I've always remembered that dream, and always remembered its important lesson that working within form, and within structure, actually makes your problems easier to solve. This is certainly true in writing, for example, where you can't hope to write a limerick if you don't know the rules of limericks: the number of lines, the rhyme scheme, and so on.

There once was a husband in Buckoff
Who told his old lady to—

Well, you know how limericks work.

What's true for limericks is true for poker night. It works better, and it's altogether more satisfying, if it has a good, strong set of rules to stand upon. In this section we'll talk about some typical "house rules" for a home poker game. Most aren't gospel, and many can be argued either way (the rule against check-and-raise betting, for example). I want to stress this point: It really doesn't matter *what* your house rules are, so long as they're clearly understood and mutually agreed upon before the start of play.

Let's start with an attitudinal rule, one of deceptively broad utility: *No whinging!* To *whinge*, if you do not know, is "to complain fretfully," or whine. You'll find whingers in all walks of poker life, and they should be elided from your home game without mercy, no matter how faithfully they donate their money, for they are plague upon poker, and their bad spirit will bring everybody down. Poker night should be a happy happenstance or, really, what's the point? If people can't sign on to the idea of "play hard, have fun, keep cool," they truly don't belong in your game. In some games, a thirty-second rule applies to all complaints and disputes: The aggrieved party is allowed to rant for half a minute, but if he continues beyond that point, he has to pay a penalty into the pot.

For your own part, never complain—even if you feel like complaining, and even if you feel like your complaint is utterly justified. Whinging won't endear you to anyone; worse, it will make you look like a loser and inspire your opponents to beat up on you, as if they were a pride of lions and you were the weakest springbok in the herd. Worst of all, your whinging will blacken your mood, and it's impossible to play winning poker in the midst of a dark glower. That's why poker author Roy West offers the practical adage: "Play happy or don't play at all."

Because this rule against whinging is so important—the K-Y

Jelly, if you will, of a well-lubricated poker game—I've included it here in graphic form, and invite you to copy, enlarge, and hand-color it, and pin it to the wall where everyone can see.

WHINGING

Violators Will Be Shot

And no, I don't think the punishment is too extreme.

Now let's move on to some more serious rules. Not all of this may be clear to you at once, but please bear with me. Whatever isn't explained in detail here will be covered later in the play-of-games section. Right now I just want to illustrate the kinds of choices you'll need to make in establishing your house rules, and to point out some of the options you have.

Buy-ins and Betting Limits. We've already discussed how to go about setting these, but you'll want to clarify for all players exactly what they're getting into. Tell them the buy-in, and say how much you're taking to defray your costs. Also spell out whether or not they have to buy in up front. You might take it as a given that it's "pay to play," but this is not always the case. In some poker games, no money actually changes hands until the game is over. The bank simply keeps track of how many chips each player has bought during the course of the evening, and the books are balanced at the end. In a $200 buy-in game, for example, if you ended up with just $90 in chips, you'd have to give the bank an additional $110 to make your buy-in right. Meanwhile, Smiley ended up with $355 in chips, but he only takes $155 in cash, his original buy-in being subtracted from his winnings.

For my money, this is an awkward way to go about running a bank, and it leads to real problems if the books don't balance at the end. *(Did Smiley take an extra buy-in that didn't get recorded? Did Frowny?)* The purpose of this "no money down" method, as I understand it, is to maintain the legal fiction that the game is not a cash game and/or to keep wads of loot out of sight in case bad guys break in. Both fears—of cops and of robbers—strike me as unrealistic and quaint. Just have your players pay as they go and you'll save yourself a tremendous amount of hassle at the end.

Betting Structures. Poker games are played either *fixed limit, spread limit, pot limit* or *no limit*. Let's briefly define each type:

Fixed limit. Like the name implies, the betting limits are fixed, at one betting unit for the first rounds of betting, and two betting units for the last rounds of betting. Games like hold'em and Omaha, for instance, each have four rounds of betting, and in a $5–10 fixed-limit version of these games you can only bet and raise in $5 increments on the first two betting rounds, and in $10 increments on the last two. In seven-card stud, to take another example, you could bet and raise $5 during the first two rounds of betting, and $10 on the last three. Most cardroom poker is played fixed limit. Many home games play a modified version of fixed limit, with a third, larger bet allowed on the final round of betting. Thus you might find a game that plays $1–2–5, where the limits are fixed at $1 and $2 for the first rounds of betting, but go up to $5 on the end. As you might imagine, this muscular last bet creates some powerful bluffing opportunities.

Spread limit. In spread-limit poker, players can bet anything between the lower and upper limits any time they like. In Las Vegas you'll typically find spread-limit $1–5 seven-card stud games, where players can bet and raise anything from $1 to $5 at any time. The rules of spread-limit betting usually require that raises and reraises on any given betting round be at least as big as the bets that preceded them. If I open for $3, for example, you typically won't be allowed to call my bet and then raise either $1 or $2. In some home games, however, players are allowed to "kill" a raise by raising for a minimum amount, even though there's been a big raise in front of them. This has the effect of putting the brakes on the action, and players with iffy hands like to have the option available to them.

In both fixed-limit and spread-limit poker, it's common practice to put a three-raise limit on every round of betting. This allows players to determine how much it will cost them to call all bets. In a $.25–.50 game with a three-raise limit, for example, you'll know that the last round of betting can't cost you more than—a bet and three raises—$2.

Pot limit. In pot-limit poker, you can bet or raise any amount up to the size of the pot. Pot limit is a tricky betting structure—so tricky that it's rarely played in home games. Even the most seasoned pot-limit players have occasional trouble determining the size of the pot and the size of allowable raises. See if you can track this target:

> Abel, Baker, and Charlie Dog are in the pot together. Abel opens for $100. Baker raises the maximum. Charlie Dog reraises the maximum. Abel and Baker both call. How much is in the pot right now?

You might need a pencil and paper to figure it out or, to visualize it better, a big stack of chips.

Abel opens for $100. If Baker wants to raise the maximum, he first puts in his $100 call. Now there's $200 in the pot, which means he can raise another $200, bringing the pot to $400. Charlie Dog calls $400—bringing the pot to $800—then reraises the maximum, another $800. Abel and Baker have to put in $1,100 and $900 respectively to call, bringing the pot total to $3,600.

Is that the answer you got? Like I said, pot limit is tricky. You rarely encounter it in home games and you probably won't play much of it at all until you're well down the path of your poker growth.

No limit. This betting structure lets you bet anything you want any time you want, regardless of the size of the pot. No-limit poker can be very adrenalating. The first time you push your chips forward and croak, "I'm all in," believe me, your heart will race. No-limit poker is very popular now, thanks to the television exposure it has lately received. Trouble is, no-limit poker is also a real chip burner. With players able to bet anything they want anytime they want, it's easy to go broke in a hurry, which tends to drive weaker players from the game.

And weaker players are the very ones we want *in* the game! The main advantage of limit poker (whether fixed limit or spread limit) is that it literally limits the amount of money players are likely to lose, allowing them to stay in action longer. It's your call, of course, but for the sake of building and sustaining a robust home game I recommend limit play, at least to start.

In setting the betting structure, you'll also want to determine whether check-and-raise betting is to be allowed. This is standard practice in cardrooms. You check, indicating weakness . . . I bet, falling into your trap . . . then you raise, getting more money into the pot. In home games, for some reason, check-raising has traditionally not been allowed. Perhaps it's considered unsportsmanlike, I don't know. In any case, it's one tradition I suggest you buck. Check-raising is a powerful piece of poker strategy, and banning it detracts from the subtlety and texture of the game.

Dealer's Choice—to a Point. Most home poker games are played *dealer's choice*, which means that as each player takes his turn dealing, he gets to say which specific poker variant is being played. He may, for example, declare, "Seven-card stud, straight high," or "Texas hold'em," or "double-draw lowball." The choice is his, and that's why it's called dealer's choice. But not all variations of poker are tolerated in all home games, and it will be up to the group to decide which games are or are not allowed.

In my home poker game (and therefore in most sensible ones), wild cards are *never* allowed, and anyone who suggests playing with them faces a hail of hooted derision. In other home games I've played in, certain variants are banned because they either don't seem like real poker or because they're too expensive. Still other home games, in an attempt to emulate cardroom poker, restrict themselves to the poker variants you'd actually find in cardrooms, and that's fine, too. Over time, the range of games tends to be self-selecting; that is, players call the games that players enjoy most. Half the fun of home poker is the variety of games played, and half the profit comes from being better at arcane games than your foes. "If you can deal it, we can play it" is not a bad way to go.

But seriously, stay away from wild cards. That's just really not poker at all.

Considerations of Low. High-only poker is completely cut-and-dried. We all know what beats what, and no matter how much you wish your straight could beat my flush, we both know that dog don't hunt. When you're playing high-low split pot games, though, a number of gray areas emerge. Your complete set of house rules will set policy on a number of matters related to the value and play of low poker hands.

Best low. As we've already discussed, in most poker realms the best possible low is 5-4-3-2-A. If you wish to establish this as your standard, simply make it clear that "wheel low is best low," and that straights and flushes do not negate the value of the low hand. If you wish to establish a different standard, that's your right, so long as everyone knows and agrees in advance.

Qualified low. In many forms of high-low poker, the low hand is only considered to be valid if it is *qualified* by containing five different cards ranked eight or lower. A low hand of 8-7-6-2-A is a qualified low, while a low hand of 9-4-3-2-A is not. Usually it's up to the dealer to declare whether the game is being played with or without a qualified low (also called *eight must*), but the house rules should speak to this point, with language, for example, like: "All high-low games require qualified lows unless the dealer specifically states otherwise."

From a strategic point of view, there are arguments to be made both for and against qualifying the lows. Unqualified lows keep more players in the pot because they figure that if their high hands don't materialize, they might be able to turn around and steal the low. On the other hand, qualified lows create the possibility of big *scoopers* (one-winner pots) when someone is going high against a bunch of low draws that never manage to qualify. Some games, like Omaha high-low split, are always played with an eight-qualified low. Other games, like seven-card stud high-low split play very well either with or without an eight must. Try it both ways and see what works for you. In the end, it really doesn't matter whether you play with qualified lows or not, so long as everyone is clear on whether the lid is on or off.

Chip-Declare or Cards Speak? Determining the winners in a split-pot game is not quite as easy as it seems. In a game like seven-card stud high-low split, your seven cards can be combined and recombined in groups of five to make your best high hand or low hand, or both. For instance, you may hold A♥-8♥-3♠-3♣-2♠-7♣-3♦, and use the 8-7-3-2-A for low and the three threes for high. Do you win both ways? If you're playing *cards speak*, all you have to do is lay down your hand and wait till they push you the pot. But in many home games, the issue is complicated by a little wrinkle called *chip-declare*.

In chip-declare games, each player determines whether he thinks his hand will win for high or for low, and signals his decision by holding a certain number of chips in his closed fist. Typically no chips in hand represents low and one equals high, though I've played in games where it's one for low and two for high. After the players' choices are revealed (the declare), those who went high compete only against the other highs, and likewise the lows compete against the lows. Now you can see why the question of a qualified low is so salient: If the low isn't qualified, you can win half the pot just by being the only person to go low, no matter what ragged hand you hold.

To complicate matters further, players have the option of going *pig*, or declaring their intention to win both the high and the low side of the pot. Pig is usually signified by two chips in hand if it's none for low and one for high, or three chips in hand if it's one for low and two for high. Now here's the thing about going pig: You must win *both* sides of the pot outright in order to scoop. If you lose, or even tie, in either direction, you're eliminated, and the pot goes to somebody else.

Who gets it? This is a matter of great debate. Say, for example, that you've declared low, I'm going high, and a third player, Oinky Oinkerson, decides to go pig. In this instance he has a better low than you have, but I have him beaten for high. Oinky is eliminated, but what about you? Are you entitled to half the pot, even though your low hand wasn't the best low? Are you, in other words, allowed to *back in* to the low, or should I, the last remaining player with a winning hand, be entitled to it all? As I said, it's a matter of great debate. My logic tells me that if the pig is eliminated, it's as if he never existed, and the pot should be split between the best remaining high and low hands respectively. Other players' logic tells them that the hero who slays the pig should be entitled to all the glory and spoils. Your logic can guide you to any decision you like, so long as you establish the rule and then stick to it consistently. Obviously this issue goes away if you're playing cards speak.

Another matter concerning chip-declare games is the order in which players declare their intention to go high or low. In most home games, everyone declares simultaneously, so that no player has the advantage of knowing what other players are doing before he has to decide. In some games, though, players declare in sequence, with the person who made the final raise before the declare being also the last person to declare high or low. Since this convention occasionally presents blatant steal opportunities— *Everyone else is going low, so I'll just go high*—it gives quite an edge to the person who made the last bet. This creates a lot of action in the final betting round, which, of course, is why it's done that way.

Finally, you'll have to decide whether or not to include a round of betting after the declare. Some games have them and some don't. The bet-after-declare is clearly advantageous to one player going low, say, while two or three others are still competing for high. That player has a *lock low*, a guaranteed win, and can bet with impunity, knowing that he's sure to profit so long as two or more players are calling bets in competition for the other half of the pot. Games without the bet after the declare tend to be less volatile, with smaller pots and less fluctuation. If you want a wide-open game, establish bet-after-declare. For a more tame game, proceed directly from declare to showdown.

These, then, are the things you have to think about in establishing rules for high-low split games:

- What's the best low?
- Will the low be qualified or unqualified?

- Cards speak or chip-declare?
- How many chips declare?
- What are the rules for pig?
- Declare simultaneously or sequentially?
- Bet or no bet after the declare?

If all of this seems like a lot of skull sweat, so much so that you'd rather stick to high-only games, *resist that urge!* High-low games are the life blood of most poker nights. The rules and procedures do take some sorting out, but it's worth the effort in terms of action and entertainment and, not least, in terms of profit for savvy players who know how to exploit the high-low edge.

Going Light or Going All-In. Cardroom poker is played *table stakes.* This means that you can only risk the money you have on the table at the start of the hand. If you have five bucks out there, the most you can lose is five bucks, but also the most you can win is five bucks times the number of players who call your five-buck bet. Home poker can also be played table stakes, but the common convention is to allow players to *go light*, borrowing money from the pot until the deal is over, when they've either won the hand and have no woes, or lost the hand and have to *make up their lights* (pay back what they owe) before the next deal begins.

Let's consider a typical poker scenario and see how it plays out differently when played *table stakes* versus *going light*. Hal O'Peño is down to his last twenty dollars, but meanwhile Anne O'Dyne and Angie O'Plasty have well over a hundred bucks each. On the first round of betting, Hal, playing table stakes, *goes all-in*, throwing his last twenty bucks in the pot. Anne and Angie call. There's sixty dollars in the pot (now called the *main pot*) and Hal is eligible to win this amount. But the hand isn't over.

Through subsequent betting rounds, Anne and Angie build a second pot, a *side pot*, for which only they two compete. When the hand is over, first Anne and Angie show their cards down. Let's say that Angie has a flush to beat Anne's straight. She wins the side pot. But back over here, Hal has a full house, so he wins the main pot. It may be much smaller than the side pot, but that's Hal's tough luck; he should have put more money on the table before the hand began.

This isn't an issue if Hal goes light. In that case, after he puts his last bet into the pot, he starts drawing bets out of the pot and stacks them neatly in front of him. In this way, we all know exactly how much Hal would have bet if he still had chips. If he wins, he'll win much more than if he'd gone all-in, but if he loses, he must immediately match his lights with cash, and hand over both the cash and the chips to the winner.

Tie Hands. Suppose in the example above that Hal and Angie had exactly the same hand, and tied for winners. There are a couple of little things to think about here. First, if Hal is light, it's an easy matter for him to pay out what he owes. All he has to do is give his stack of lights to Angie, after which they split between them the chips that remain in the pot. Second, it occasionally happens that there will be an extra, indivisible chip in the pot. I have long tried to convince my fellow home poker players that the extra chip should go to the best-looking player (me) or the baldest one (me again), but they have not been moved. Persuasive nonsense aside, standard practice dictates that the extra chip goes to the player closest to the dealer's left. If there's an odd chip in a split between the high hand and the low hand, the high hand gets it regardless of relative seat position. As an alternative, the odd chip can be *rolled over*, left in the pot for the next hand.

Antes. If you've played any home poker at all, you're no doubt familiar with the incredible pain-in-the-ass hassle over who's paid their ante and who has not. Hand after hand it continues, to the point where I've actually seen grown men come to blows over whether that half-dollar chip in the pot came out of Rudy's stack or Rudi's. While I understand the logic of the ante—it loosens up play by getting the pot started and putting something out there for someone to win—I've had it up to here with the incessant chirping of "Ante up! Ante up!" and the constant need to badger forgetful (or skinflint) players into putting up their share. There has to be a better way. Well, guess what? There is.

In my home game, we long ago adopted the convention that "dealer antes for the table." Whenever it's your turn to deal, you just put in the normal ante multiplied by the number of players in the game. If everyone in an eight-handed game would otherwise have anted a quarter, the dealer posts a total of two dollars for all. It's convenient and simple, and in the long run everyone pays the same amount as if they'd anted individually all along.

Some poker variations, like hold'em and Omaha, are not played with antes in the first place, and so it may not seem to make sense for a dealer who's calling hold'em to be anteing for the table as well. We'll talk more about hold'em and Omaha, and their convention of blind (or forced) bets, but for the sake of consistency just do this: *Have the dealer ante for the table every time he holds the deck.* That way there will never be any confusion and there will always be something in the pot worth shooting for.

Misdeals. Maurice is dealing. Teddy picks up his cards and is delighted to find four of a kind. Trouble is, Mikey picks up his cards and finds he has one too many. And Worm has one too few. A misdeal is declared and, Teddy's bitching notwithstanding, the cards come back. Misdeals are an inevitable reality of player-dealt poker games, and the best thing I can tell you about it is *get over it*. Shit, as they say, happens.

Some misdeals don't matter. If I accidentally deal an extra card to a player and he hands it back without looking at it . . . no harm, no foul. But what if cards are exposed? Most cardrooms will tolerate one exposed card, but not two. That is, if one card is accidentally revealed, it's discarded and a new card dealt, but once a second card is exposed, a whole new deal is required. Beyond exposed cards, the other type of misdeal you typically see is when a player has too many or too few cards. If the player has too few cards, I see nothing wrong with filling him in from the top of the deck. If he has too many, though, and he has looked at them, then technically his hand is dead, even though the fault is not his own. In my home game, we split the difference. If the player discovers that he has too many cards before anyone else has acted, then we just deal over. But if someone, even someone in front of him, has already opened the betting, sad to say, he's going to have to throw in his hand and wait for the next deal.

Home games tend to be a little loose with these procedures, and my own rule of thumb on the subject is similarly fuzzy: If the mistake is instantly and easily corrected, with no player having extra information, I say go ahead and fix it; if the fix is not automatic, or there's any doubt or dispute, just deal the darn thing over. But the area of misdeals is one where it really helps to have a firm hand and the courage of your convictions. *Someone* is bound to be upset, either the player whose hand was killed or the player who had terrific cards called back by a misdeal. If the house rules are clear and consistent on this issue, then both players can be referred to . . .

WHINGING

Violators Will Be Shot

. . . and play can continue.

One thing we do in our home game, and you might do in yours, is make the dealer pay for his mistakes. In our game, if you screw up the deal, you "pay the pot" an amount equal to the ante you've already posted for the table. The most important thing is to just not get bent out of shape. If we can't all play nicely, they might not let us play at all.

Here, then, is a typical set of house rules for a modestly staked home poker game. You don't have to do it this way, but if you do, you won't go too far wrong.

JV's House Rules

BUY-IN	$100 gets you $90 in chips plus food and drink.
BETTING LIMITS	$1 or $2 at any time; $4 on the last round of betting only.
THREE RAISE LIMIT	One bet and three raises are allowed during each betting round. Check-raising is allowed.
TYPES OF GAMES	Dealer's choice; no wild cards.
BEST LOW	Wheel low is best low.
EIGHT MUST	Unless otherwise stated by the dealer, in all high-low split the low must qualify.
CHIP-DECLARE	All players declare simultaneously. One chip in hand is low. Two chips in hand is high. Three chips in hand is pig. No bet after the declare.
PIG RULE	If you declare both high and low, you must win both sides outright to win the pot; ties count as a loss.
BACK-IN RULE	If a player goes pig and is eliminated, the remaining players with the best high and best low split the pot, regardless of whom the pig might have beaten.
GOING LIGHT	Going light is allowed, but the player must make up his lights immediately upon completion of the hand.
TIE HANDS	Tie hands split the pot; the extra chip, if any, goes to the closest player on the dealer's left.
ANTES	Dealer antes for the table.
MISDEALS	Second exposed card equals misdeal; incorrect hands can only be corrected before any action has been taken.
CREDIT	No credit extended; bring more money next time.
THE HOUSE RULES	Decision of the house is final; no exceptions; no whinging.

Okay, there you have it: a good, strong set of rules. But remember, this is only a starting point. After all, Elvis wasn't right about everything (drugs and eating habits come immediately to mind) and sometimes the rules *do* confine. Though your poker peers will thank you for being forceful in stating the rules, you must also be flexible, and willing to adjust the rules to the whims, and the will, of the group. If you're too autocratic, you may just end up playing alone. So always make room for the new idea. Except for wild cards. You gotta draw the line somewhere.

5

BASIC POKER GAMES

♠

In this chapter, we'll examine some of the most popular poker variations that you'll find in (or want to introduce to) the home games in which you play. You probably already know some of these games, and if you do, feel free to skip ahead to the strategy sections. But keep this text handy for your home games, for disputes do arise and it will be nice to have an authority on hand (even one so shamelessly self-appointed as *moi*) to settle them. "Can you draw four cards to an ace in draw poker?" "Well, *Vorhaus* says . . ."

First, another *tiny* word about procedure, and then I promise, *promise*, that we'll get down to the games. I mentioned earlier that you'll want to have two decks on hand, so that one can be prepared while the other is in play. Here's how that should work. If I'm dealing, the player sitting behind me (that is, to my right) should be shuffling the deck we used on the last hand. He places it on his left when he's done, so that I can take it and pass it to my left at the start of the next hand. I cut the deck toward the new dealer, who completes the cut and can now call the game and deal the cards. Meanwhile, I'm shuffling the deck from the last hand and getting it ready for the next. Simple, right?

Okay, let's get to the games.

♦ ♦ ♦ Draw Poker

Draw poker is the granddaddy of all poker games, but a granddaddy on life support. This might surprise you since, after all, draw poker is drenched in American blood. Its pedigree stretches back to riverboats and Deadwood saloons and the Western movies of our youth. It's the first poker game almost all of us learned. It taught us what beats what.

But almost no one plays it anymore. Why? No action. You either have a good hand or you don't, and sensible players quickly learn to fold bad hands. An action game, and there are plenty of them as we will see, is one where even sensible players don't fold bad hands. Plus, draw poker offers only two rounds of betting, compared to four rounds in such games as hold'em and Omaha, five in seven-card stud, and even more in some of the crazier home poker games you'll find. Draw poker, then, is like a stiff oldster in bow tie and starched white shirt while all the kids around him are wearing hip-hop logo wear and baggy pants pulled down with their underwear exposed.

That said, it *is* a game that everyone knows, so let's spend a moment living, as it were, in the past.

The Basic Game. Draw poker, also known as *five-card draw*, starts with each player putting in an ante or, per preference, with the dealer anteing for the table. The dealer then deals every player five cards facedown. Players look at their cards (taking care not to flash their hand to prying eyes on the left or right) and a round of betting takes place. The first player to the left of the dealer has the option of *checking* (betting no money) or placing a bet according to the betting structure of the game. If the first player checks, the second player may check as well, but once someone has placed a bet—opened the pot—checking is no longer an option. You either have to call the bet or raise or fold. Action moves around the table clockwise until everyone has called all the bets and raises or folded their hand.

After the first round of betting comes the *draw*, at which time players can discard the cards they don't want and replace them with, they hope, cards that improve their hand. How many cards can each player draw? This is either the dealer's decision or a subject covered by the house rules, but in any case you need to make sure that there are enough cards to go around. It has long been a convention of draw poker in home games that players can draw three cards, "or four with an ace," meaning that if you have an ace you can, by showing it, earn the right to replace your other four cards. This may be allowed, but it's bad strategy for two reasons. First, everyone else knows one of your cards. Second, you're getting four new random cards at a time when anyone with even a lowly pair of deuces has a better hand than you. Still, people do draw four to an ace; you may allow it if you choose, just don't do it yourself.

After the draw there's another round of betting, starting with the first still-in-action player to the dealer's left. In fixed-limit poker, the size of bets and raises during this round is exactly double the size of the pre-draw bets and raises. If someone bets and everyone else folds, that player claims the pot. Otherwise, once the betting is complete all active players turn over their hands and the winner is determined according to the sacred canon of *what beats what*.

Variations. Draw poker is sometimes played with a joker, or *bug*, in the deck. This card is not exactly wild: It can't be used for absolutely anything, but it can be used as an ace, or to complete a straight or a flush. If you're drawing to J♥-T♥-9♥-joker, any king, queen, eight, seven, or heart will complete your hand. Draw an ace and you have two aces, but draw another ten, say, and you have only a pair of tens, not the trip tens you'd have if the joker were completely wild. Draw poker and lowball (*see below*) are the only cardroom poker games where you'll see anything like a wild card being used.

A popular variation of draw poker is *jacks or better*, in which you can only open the pot with a hand containing a pair of jacks or more. If no one has these so-called *openers*, everyone antes again, and new cards are dealt. Obviously this is a case where all the players, and not just the dealer, must chip in; otherwise, no dealer in his right mind would ever call the game. The jacks-or-better convention assures that battles aren't fought over trash, but over at least semidecent hands.

Another version of this game is *jacks progressive*, in which players have to open for jacks or better on the first deal, but if no one has openers, the minimum requirement is raised to queens or better on the next round. If there's still no opener, on the next deal the minimum goes up to kings . . . then aces . . . then back to jacks. With everyone throwing in an ante on each new deal, the pot can get quite large by the time someone finally finds a hand to play.

Don't like progressive? Try *jacks back to lowball* or more familiarly *jacks back*. In this game, if no one has minimum openers, the hand is played for the best low instead of the best high. I suppose the thinking is that if the quality high cards are absent, quality low cards must be out there instead.

And finally we have *jacks to open, trips to win*. As the name implies, the winning hand must be trips—three of a kind—or better. If no one has winners, a new hand is dealt—but only to players who haven't previously folded. This is a real action game because players who have no kind of hand at all will still call bets both before and after the draw, rather than fold and be eliminated from play. They cling to the fervent hope that none of their foes has a qualified winning hand and they'll get a shot at the pot on a subsequent deal.

This is a variation of draw poker that allows strong players to exploit weak ones, so let's pause and talk strategy for a second.

There's a concept in poker called *chasing*. When you don't have the best hand but you have hopes of catching up, you're said to be chasing. Often it makes sense to chase. If the pot is large and the cost of calling a bet is small, and if your chances of improving your hand are reasonably good, then chasing has what's known as a *positive expectation*. Other times, though, chasing has a *negative expectation*—sometimes quite a large one. Recall the proposition we considered earlier where a fifty-fifty coin flip offered less than a fifty-fifty return. That's negative expectation. Any time you can get someone to chase with a negative expectation, they're making a mistake, and you stand to profit from that mistake.

So now let's look at this business of jacks to open, trips to win. You have two players, Chip and Dale. Chip only calls when he has a big pair, two pair, four to a flush, or open-ended straight, or better. But Dale calls with any old hand, even one that has no reasonable chance of improving to a qualified winner. Why does Dale do this? Because he *just can't stand* to surrender the pot to Chip without a fight. And why is it such a big mistake? Because Dale is chasing in the fog. He's basing his hope of success not on this hand but on the *next* hand—a hand he'll get to see only if Chip fails to get to trips or better. We're back to the business of the horse race. Dale enter every race, but Chip only participates when he has a big head start. You don't need to do the math to see Chip's huge advantage. If Chip and Dale each play their respective strategies long enough, Chip will own Dale's house, car, and big-screen TV.

So now we come to a magic word for strategic success in poker. It's such an important word that I'm going to put it in a fancy typeface and set it off in a space by itself. Here's the word.

FOLD!

Yep. *Fold*. Just fold. If you fold your bad hands more often than your opponents fold theirs, you will be a home poker winner, I promise.

Is that really all it takes? Just playing tighter than the next guy? Well, yes and no. The most common mistake that most players make is playing too many hands—and sticking with their losers too long. If you give yourself the knowledge and the discipline to stay out of negative expectation situations, you'll evade that mistake and instantly place yourself ahead of the usual poker night pack. But if all I taught you was *play tight*, I wouldn't be doing my job and you wouldn't be making the most of your poker-profit opportunities. So let's just consider *fold* to be the first word in a lifelong course of poker study.

Now let's move on from draw poker to the game that currently occupies the apex of poker popularity. Ladies and gentlemen, I give you . . .

♦ ♦ ♦ Texas Hold'em

The beauty of *Texas hold'em* is its deceptive simplicity. Every player gets two cards to call his own, plus five faceup cards in the middle . . . community cards that everyone shares. The object of the game is to make the best five-card hand out of the seven available. Hold'em, like golf, Zen meditation, and certain acts of sexual congress, takes five minutes to learn and a lifetime to master.

In virtually every cardroom in America, if they have any poker at all, they have hold'em. In virtual cardrooms online, hold'em predominates. If you've seen any poker on television in the last few years, it's a lead-pipe cinch you've seen hold'em. No-limit hold'em—the so-called "Cadillac of poker"—is the featured event at all major poker tournaments.

And yet the game was not widely known outside of Texas and a few Nevada outposts before the mid-1980s. Why did hold'em take off? What makes the game so popular? The answer, I think, lies in its delicate balance between luck and skill. Lucky players win often enough to keep coming back—and skillful players are there waiting for them when they do. In other words, the perception is that you have to be lucky to win at hold'em, but the reality is you have to be skilled. It's this beautiful gap between perception and reality that makes hold'em what it is: far and away, contemporary America's poker game of choice.

The Basic Game. In Texas hold'em, each player gets two cards to start. There's a round of betting, and then three cards are turned over in the middle of the table. These cards (collectively called *the flop*) are common cards or community cards; they're part of everybody's hand. Let's say you start with an ace and a king of clubs (A♣-K♣) and hit this flop:

Your hand so far is a pair of aces with a king *kicker*, or sidecard (your king being your kicker here). Your opponent, Slim Panatella, meanwhile, started with a pair of queens (Q-Q) and now has only two queens with an ace kicker. At this point, you're *in boss command* (ahead in the hand). After the flop, there's a second round of betting. Then another community card, called the *turn card*, is revealed. If the turn is a queen, whoa, Nelly!

You still have your pair of aces, but Slim has improved to three queens. However, between the two clubs in your hand and the two on board, you now have four clubs . . . a flush draw. There's one more card to come. Just for fun, see if you can count how many of the remaining cards will give you the best hand. Don't forget to consider the cards that would improve your hand but improve Slim's as well.

You have eight outs left in the deck. All nine remaining clubs will give you a flush, but the 9♣ would also give Slim a full house, thus flushing your flush. Likewise, the A♥ or A♦ would improve your hand to trip aces, but push Slim past you to a winning full house of three queens and two aces, or *queens full*.

All of these thoughts pass quickly through your mind (and if they pass slowly now, don't worry, for the speed of such ruminations will swiftly increase) while you and Slim engage in a third round of betting, after which the fifth community card, the *river card*, is placed on the board. Alas for you, it's a *brick*, an unhelpful card, and the final board reads . . .

Now there's a final round of betting, in which you would call or raise, if you thought you had the best hand, or fold if you figured Slim had you beat. As in draw poker, the last round is followed by the showdown, where the winner is determined.

To get the hang of hold'em just deal yourself a bunch of two-card hands and lay out a bunch of flops, turns, and rivers. You'll quickly come to see that high cards are highly prized in hold'em, because they make hands containing high pairs or high two-pairs or sometimes, as in the case of a naked ace, win with no help at all from the board. Suited cards also have value because they become flushes, as, similarly, connected cards such as J-T (jack-ten) have a head start toward straights. A hand that's both suited and con-nected, such as 8♦-7♦, has two-way potential for growth, and big *suited connectors* like K♣-Q♣ can turn into straights *or* flushes *or* big pairs or *sets* (three of a kind). The best starting hands are pairs, and the best pair of all is A-A. Starting with *pocket aces* is no guar-antee of a win, but if you had your druthers, you'd take that hand every time.

Unlike draw and stud poker, which call for antes, and can be covered by the dealer-ante convention we've already discussed, Texas hold'em and other so-called flop games start the action with one or two forced bets, called *blinds*. The reason for blinds is the same as for any forced bet: to get the action started. With-out the blinds, there would be nothing in the pot to win, and so no incentive for any player to join the fray without a truly top hand.

In a typical fixed-limit Texas hold'em game, the person to the dealer's left is called the *small blind*. He has to post a blind bet half the size of the lower limit bet for that game. The next player to the left, the *big blind*, puts up a bet equal to one lower limit bet. In a $2–4 fixed-limit hold'em game, then, the small blind posts a $1 bet and the big blind puts up $2. Here's a look at the blinds' positions relative to the dealer.

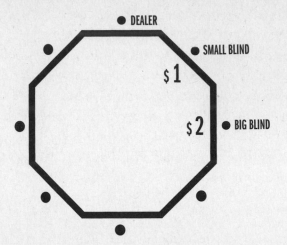

Because of the blinds in hold'em and other flop games, the first round of betting functions a little differently from later rounds. After the *hole cards* are dealt, the blinds are not the first players to act. That job falls to the first player to the left of the big blind, the player *under the gun*. His options are to call a bet the size of the big blind, or raise to twice the size of the big blind, or fold. Each player in turn acts behind him until the action comes back around to the blinds, who, in the first round only, are last to act. After the flop and for all subsequent rounds of betting, the first live player to the left of the dealer, whether the blind or not, is first to act.

Obviously it would be unfair for the same players to have to pay the blinds on every hand. Not only that, position is very important in flop games like hold'em. The later you get to act, the more information you have about the relative strength of the players in front of you. Information is power in poker, so the players late or last to act have the greatest positional advantage, and players in or near the blinds have the least. That's why the deal rotates, passing one position clockwise with each new hand. As the deal moves, the blinds move with it, resulting in all players taking their fair share of the blinds and the subsequent early, middle, and late positions.

And so it goes . . . two cards in your hand, three cards on the flop, then one on the turn and one on the river. Make your best five-card hand out of seven. Bet, raise, reraise, call. Showdown, shuffle, deal. Late position, middle position, early position, big blind, small blind, dealer button, then late position once again, and the wheel goes around and around and around. If poker is po-etry, then hold'em is haiku.

> *Fierce hope of two cards*
> *in hand plus five on the board.*
> *Busted flush, oh well.*

Variations. Texas hold'em is occasionally played high-low split, eight must. In this version, the high and low hands split the pot, so long as the low is qualified with five different cards valued eight or lower. Some people modify the high-low game by dealing each player three cards to start. This version, for reasons I can't begin to imagine, is called *pineapple hold'em*, and it, in turn, has two sub-variations. In *crazy pineapple*, players get three cards to start, but must discard one of the three after the flop. In *lazy pineapple*, you keep all three cards until the end, and may use them in any com-bination of zero, one, or two cards to make your best hand. You can also use different cards for high and low, which puts a pre-mium on highly flexible hands, and especially on the ace, which plays both high and low.

If you're playing lazy pineapple, for example, you might find yourself holding A♥-J♥-J♣ and facing a final board of J♠-2♣-4♣-8♥-6♦. Your best high hand, requiring the use of both jacks in your hand, would be three jacks with an eight kicker, not three jacks with an ace kicker because you can't use all three cards from your hand. Your best low would be 8-6-4-2-A, requiring the use of just one hole card, the ace. Would you win both ways? Your high looks pretty good; you can only lose to a straight. Your low, though, is in jeopardy because while you're only using one card from your hand, your foes may be using two. Someone holding A-3, for example, has 6-4-3-2-A, the *nut low*, or best possible low hand.

If that's not quite enough quirkiness for you, there's another version of hold'em called *reverse hold'em*, where the community cards are revealed one-one-three, instead of the normal three-one-one, with the usual round of betting between each reveal. There's even *hump hold'em*, where the cards come one-three-one. As you can see, there's no shortage of inventiveness in the poker universe, and one of the true blessings of home poker is that prevailing "If you can deal it, we can play it" attitude. You certainly won't find this attitude in cardrooms, where they spread the games they spread and your choices are limited to the proffered fare. So with home hold'em, as with all forms of poker, feel free to stretch your imagination, for today's flight of fancy may be tomorrow's staple game.

However, if you're thinking of inventing a four-card version of hold'em, you can save your effort, for that game already exists, and it's called . . .

♦ ♦ ♦ Omaha

It may seem weird, but we're going to discuss Omaha in reverse order, first considering high-low split Omaha and then looking at the high-only version of the game. There's a reason for this, just like there's a reason for everything. Except yawning. I never have understood why people yawn. Or why when we see someone else yawn, we yawn, too. In fact, sometimes the mere mention of the word *yawn* can make people yawn. It might have made you yawn right now, or maybe that's just this tangent I'm off on.

Anyway, Omaha: We're looking at high-low split first because it's just wildly more popular than high-only. In cardrooms across America, high-low Omaha is second only in prevalence to hold'em (or perhaps third after seven-card stud), while straight high Omaha is almost nowhere to be seen. Over in Europe, interestingly, high-only Omaha, especially pot-limit Omaha, is the game of choice. One could pause to wonder (or even stop to investigate) how a game named after a Midwestern American city became the game of choice in European card clubs, but if we're going down that road, we might as well bring up yawning again, and we've already seen where that leads.

The Basic Game. The formal name for the game is Omaha high-low split, eight or better for low, but that's kind of clunky, so many people use the shorthand handle Omaha/8. As you already know, when we speak of "eight or better for low," we mean that the winning low hand must contain five separate cards valued eight or lower. If there is no qualified low, then the high hand scoops the pot.

A reminder: In Omaha/8, as in all low-hand poker variations, the highest low card always determines the strength of the low. If two high cards are tied, then the second-highest card decides the winner, and so on down the line. Thus the low hand 7-5-4-3-A beats 8-5-4-3-A, and 6-5-4-3-A barely squeaks past 6-5-4-3-2. Straights and flushes, as we've already determined, don't kill the low.

Omaha/8 is structured like hold'em: Each player gets his own hole cards to start, and players post a small and big blind to start the action. There's a round of betting, and then the flop, revealing three cards. After another round of betting, you see the turn card. Again you bet, and then comes the river card. After a final round of betting, the hands are shown, and the best high hand splits the pot with the best low hand, if any qualifies.

But here's the twist, and it's such a vital twist that I'm going to put it in a self-important little box.

> In Omaha, unlike hold'em, you get four starting cards instead of two, but you must use two cards from your hand and three from the board. Two and three. No more. No less. Two from your hand, three from the board. Forever and always. Two from your hand, three from the board!

Never forget this rule, or one day you'll find yourself thinking that the four eights you've been dealt is a winning hand. It's not. It's not even playable. Not in Omaha/8.

But don't worry if you forget the rule. Everyone does at least once.

At this point you might do yourself the favor of dealing out some four-card Omaha hands and taking a look at all the different two-card combinations that confront you. You'll quickly see that almost every hand offers the potential of at least *some* kind of draw. This, folks, is the real secret of Omaha/8's popularity: It's the ultimate action game, because everything looks like something, at least a little. Just contemplate a holding like A♠-3♣-K♠-

K♣. Those four cards taken two at a time offer the possibility of a low straight (with the A-3), a high straight (with the A-K), two different flush draws (in spades and clubs), and a pair of kings that could grow into trips or even quads. Plus the A-3 is a reasonable low draw. Rare is the *Omaholic* who could get away from this hand, and that's why it's an action game.

Since cards speak in Omaha/8, when the hand is over everyone just turns over their cards to see who won. This is a boon because with so many two-card combinations to sort through, it's often difficult to tell (at first glance and without some experience) who has the best hand or hands. Consider: Smelly Shelly holds A♦-2♠-3♣-4♥, while her archrival Ratty Patty holds T♠-J♦-8♥-7♥, and the final board shows:

Shelly thinks she's sitting pretty with the nut low of 5-4-3-2-A. She has forgotten the cardinal rule of Omaha—*two from the hand, three from the board*—and only after the showdown does she realize that there is no possible low—again because there must be three different cards on the board that are eight or lower. Meanwhile, Patty's using the T-8 from her hand and the Q-J-9 from the board to compose herself a nice little straight. But hang on, what's this? Shelly was so focused on her low that she didn't notice her 2-3 suited in spades. Now those two cards *do* play, connecting with the three spades on the board to make the lowest possible flush. Tiny, yes, but big enough to give Shelly the whole pot.

Two from your hand, three from the board, and keep your eye

on all the combinations. Even the most experienced Omaha/8 players overlook something sometimes. So don't.

Also don't overlook *Murphy's Law of Omaha*, which warns us that: "If there's a hand out there that *could* beat you, it *will* beat you." This is especially true in home games, where players cling to slim draws with high hopes. After the turn, you might be holding the *nut flush* (the best possible flush), but if the board pairs on the end, suddenly anyone who had trips now has a full house and your nut flush is nutmeat. We'll talk more about this in the strategy section, but for now just know this: If you're planning to play much Omaha/8, prepare for a bumpy ride.

Variations. In Ventura, California, there's a little cardroom called the Player's Club where they play a deviant version of Omaha/8 called *big* O. Big O plays just like regular Omaha/8, except that every player starts out with *five* cards instead of four. If you think the action is wacky and the possibilities mind-boggling with four-card Omaha, try dealing a few hands of big O. I'm not saying your head will explode, but then again it might. You can also, as with hold'em, deal *reverse Omaha* or *hump Omaha*, if you're totally perverse.

Or not even if you're totally perverse. Maybe if you just want to get some edge. It's axiomatic in poker that *those with more knowledge and expertise than their foes make money in the margin.* If you spend some time investigating, or devising, a certain poker variation before you introduce it into your home game, you'll have an exploitable advantage until your cronies get the hang of the game. Are you taking unfair advantage of them by this? Of course you are! Get over it. They didn't drive all the way from Pacoima to fold, but *you* didn't drive all the way from Pacoima to lose.

I want to pause and dwell on this for a moment, for it's an example of something I promised earlier: that you can appear to be a lovable loser while secretly exploiting and manipulating your foes to the benefit of your bankroll. Here you seem to be doing the game a favor by introducing an intriguing new style of poker. But since the style isn't entirely new to you—you've at least dealt yourself a bunch of sample hands and have a sense of their relative strength—you have a leg up on the others.

You'll see this principle in action the first time you deal Omaha/8. Players who are unaware of Murphy's Law of Omaha will routinely draw to second-best hands, and won't stop doing so until cumulative harsh evidence trims their sails. So do liven up your home game by routinely introducing new poker variants— just make sure they're less new to you than to everyone else.

Now we come to *straight high Omaha*. This game is just Omaha/8 without the low. As you might imagine, the better high Omaha hands are ones with cards in the top of the deck, especially big pairs, and high straight and flush draws. As you might further imagine, this game holds less appeal to typical home gamesters because so many hands are clearly not playable (and therefore not fun). If you're holding 2-4-9-K *rainbow* (unsuited) in high Omaha, you pretty much have to toss that piece of cheese in the muck. High-low players, though, could at least cling to the dream of hitting the nut low with a board of ace, three, and any five, six, seven, or eight. It's this dream that makes the crowd clamor for Omaha/8.

High-only Omaha, though, is not without its challenges, and not without its fans. The pot-limit variation is especially alluring to action players who love the recurring best-hand-versus-best-draw confrontations in the game. It often happens that someone has top set, for example, while his opponent has a fat draw to a straight or a flush. Since pot limit allows you to bet anything you want up to the size of the pot, the player on the draw will face a tough choice if his opponent comes after him with a pot-size bet. Pot-limit Omaha is a good way to learn how to sweat.

♦ ♦ ♦ Stud Poker

Question: If you were in San Francisco in 1963 and considering either: *A)* dropping acid or *B)* playing seven-card stud, which activity would have been illegal? Answer: *B)* seven-card stud. Until the late 1980s, though draw poker and lowball were legal in California, all forms of so-called "stud-horse" poker were not. The use of LSD, meanwhile, was outlawed in California with the passage of the Grunsky Bill in 1966. I only mention this in case you ever one day build a time machine and want to go back to California in the early '60s and not get in trouble with the law.

The Basic Game. *Five-card stud* and *seven-card stud* play pretty much the same except for the number of cards you get and the number of rounds you bet. In five-stud, after the ante (or dealer ante) every player is dealt one hidden card and one upcard (called the *hole card* and *door card* respectively), while in seven-stud, you see two hole cards and one door card to start. In cardrooms, the person with the lowest door card is the one who starts the action, with a minimum forced bet or *bring-in*. If two players have the same low card by rank, the bet is forced upon the lowest by suit. Clubs are lowest, then diamonds, hearts, and spades, just like in bridge. This is the only instance I'm aware of in poker where suits matter.

I don't know why I'm even talking about all this, though, since the convention in most home games is to start the action with the high card, not the low. Why is it done differently at home? In card-rooms, the forced bring-in from the low hand has the same function as the blinds in hold'em—it stimulates the action. In home games, where everyone came to play in the first place, stimulating the action is not a problem; hence, they let the best hand bet. If two or more players have the same high door card, the person nearest to the dealer's left is the first to act and everyone plays in turn clockwise from there. After the bet, another card is dealt, followed by more rounds of betting and dealing until all remaining players have five cards, with one hidden and four revealed. After that comes the showdown and the winner's ritual cry of: "Push the sherbet to Herbert!" or "Pass the melon to Helen!" (What can I tell you? Poker players say nutty things.)

With four rounds of betting, five-stud lends itself easily to the structure of fixed-limit poker, with the lower denomination bet allowed on the first two rounds of betting, and the upper denomination bet mandated for the last two rounds. Seven-stud is slightly trickier, because there are five betting rounds in all: one after the first three cards are dealt, then one more after, respectively, the fourth, fifth, and sixth cards, all dealt faceup, and the seventh card, dealt facedown. Most home games allow the higher-limit bet only after the fifth card (also known as *fifth street*) unless someone has an open pair on an earlier street, in which case the larger bet is allowed. Obviously in spread-limit games, where any size bet is allowed at any time, these restrictions don't apply.

In community-card games like hold'em, it's easy to determine what the best possible hand might be. If, for example, there are no pairs on board, then *full boats*—full houses—are impossible, and a flush or straight or even trips would be the boss command hand. In stud, and especially seven-stud, it's not quite so cut-and-dried. It's possible for a player to have a completely concealed full boat (known in our game as a *U-boat*) with four upcards of, say, a seven, jack, ten, and king, but a pair of tens and a king in the hole. That's why you want to pay attention to the other players' hands as they develop. Suppose Clueless Joe starts with a low club as his door card. Does he get all excited when a high club comes on fourth street? Put him on a flush draw—and proceed with caution if one of his next two cards is a club.

Seven-stud is generally more popular than five-stud simply because you more frequently see bigger hands. For example, to start with a pair of aces is huge—and rare—in five-stud, where your starting cards must match. Your odds against that specific start are 220–1. In seven-stud, where you only need to find two aces out of three starting cards, you'll have that magic hand roughly three times more frequently, once every 75 hands or so. But don't hold your breath waiting to start with three aces *(trips, rolled-up)* in seven-stud. You'll go more than 5,500 hands, on average, before that happens.

We'll discuss specific strategies later, but for now just keep in mind our familiar horse-race analogy. Play only hands that start strong or improve quickly, and make your money betting against the hopeful masses whose only starting requirement is, well, cards.

Variations. Both seven-stud and five-stud can be played high-low as well as high-only, and these variations are quite popular with home game players because, as with Omaha/8, the chance of winning half a pot doubles players' enthusiasm for jumping into the fray. In cardrooms, seven-stud is typically played cards speak, with an eight-qualified low, though in home games you'll find it played without a qualifier and with a chip-declare just about as often. Five-stud high-low is rarely played with a qualified low because you'd have to catch five perfect cards to make a qualified low, and even the most cockeyed optimist will recognize that his hand is dead for low as soon as he bricks out with any card nine or higher.

To overcome this problem of the lows drawing dead (and thus losing interest), five-stud is often played with a *twist*, or replacement card. After five cards have been dealt and bet upon, each player in turn has the option of getting rid of one of his cards and replacing it with a fresh card from the deck. Usually you have to pay for the privilege, at a price set by the dealer before the hand begins. The twist offers the promise of repairing busted draws and thus keeps the aforementioned cockeyed optimists in the game.

Let's suppose that Cicero is holding (3)-2-5-7 (where the card in parentheses represents his hole card). On fifth street, he bricks out with a jack. He'll fold, right? Not necessarily—not if he can still twist to his low. He'll call bets on fifth street, and then pay to twist, all in the stubborn hope of winning half the pot. *Half!*

Seneca, meanwhile, holds (K)-J-Q-K before the last card is dealt. It doesn't even matter what he gets, because he's already a lock for high—Cicero can't twist any card that would improve his hand past Seneca's. The best big C can do is hope to hit his low, which he'll succeed in doing less than half the time. In this instance, Seneca is *free rolling* for both sides of the pot. This is the sort of situation you want to put yourself in as frequently as possible on poker night.

Remember: It really doesn't matter whether or not Cicero hits his hand this time. *Confirmation bias* (our tendency to notice or remember outcomes we're looking for or interested in) will lead Cicero to believe that he makes his low much more often than he actually does, and if he's not getting a sufficient payout from the pot—not betting with the best of it—it's a bad gamble for Cicero, regardless of this particular (or any particular) outcome.

Consider the case of spiny Pliny. He's been watching Cicero for some time, and one thing he's come to realize is: *Cicero loves his draws.* Give Cicero three to a straight or three to a flush in seven-card stud, and he'll be in there till the end, no matter how unfavorable the odds or insufficient the payout. What does Pliny do with this knowledge? He raises! He raises a lot. His goal is to drive out the other players and get *heads up* (one-on-one) against Cicero, who is rarely as much as a fifty-fifty shot to complete his straight or flush, but who will happily (or ignorantly) accept an even-money return on his investment.

Sadly for Pliny, Plutarch has been paying attention, too. He knows how much Pliny loves to go one-on-one against Cicero, and he knows the reason why. He also knows that Pliny, in his eagerness to isolate poor Cicero, will bet hands that aren't particularly strong. Plutarch won't fold when Pliny raises—but he won't necessarily reraise either. He'll just call along, waiting to trap both the unsuspecting Cicero and the overeager Pliny with the hidden strength of his hand.

Wheels within wheels, right? Pliny behaves a certain way because of what Cicero does, and Plutarch behaves a certain way because of what Pliny does. So now Pliny needs a strategy for Plutarch and a strategy for Cicero, and also some way to make those strategies mesh. Sophocles, meanwhile, is off to one side watching all this, and he's planning his moves, too. Pliny now finds himself wondering, *Does Sophocles know what I'm doing? And if he does, does he know that I know that he knows? If he knows that I know that he knows, he'll do something different, but if he knows that I know that he knows that I know, then he'll do something altogether else.* That way, as any classical philosopher-slash-poker player will tell you, lies madness.

So let's boil it down. For success in stud-style poker or, really, in any style poker, just follow these two simple steps. First, *pay attention*. If you do this, you'll immediately set yourself apart and above the multitude of players whose thinking about poker never advances past Cicero's proto-strategy of: Cards! Play! Next, *pay attention to those who pay attention*. Know which of your foes are crafty, and avoid mixing it up with them. To put it more didactically . . .

Rule Book Don't challenge strong players. Challenge weak ones. That's what they're there for.

♦ ♦ ♦ Lowball

What's the difference between an optimist and a pessimist? An optimist looks at the glass and says, "It's half full." A pessimist looks at the glass and says, "If I drink this, I'll probably spill it all over myself and ruin my shirt." This sort of dank depressive thinking is well known in gaming circles. It's the same thinking that leads dice players to bet the *don't* or dark side of the craps proposition. And it is this "If I never get good cards, I might as well try for bad ones" mind-set that leads to the popularity of low draw poker or *lowball*.

The Basic Game. In lowball, as in five-card draw, everyone gets five cards face down, and each player may trade in his stiffs for new cards after the first betting round—drawing, however, to low hands rather than high. Lowball is usually played with a blind or two to stimulate the action, and obviously it's not necessary to qualify for the low, since only the low hand wins the pot, with no split to the high.

Lowball players are a breed apart. Devious by nature, they make steely bluffs like raising before the draw, taking no cards (regardless of the cards they hold) and then betting again after the draw. They want you to think that they started out with a *pat hand*, one that needed no improvement, and since they drew no cards, you might just believe them. It's certainly much easier to make a pat low than a pat high hand, which means that both good hands and good bluffs are more common in lowball than in five-card draw.

In fixed-limit lowball, bets are a single unit before the draw and a double unit after the draw. Since there are only two rounds of betting, and since there's only one winner, the pots in lowball tend to be smaller than in other poker variations. This doesn't mean it's not a good game. If you're an extremely negative person, it might be just your cup of hemlock.

Variations. In California cardrooms and elsewhere, lowball is frequently played with a joker, which may substitute for any card without restriction. As you might imagine, anyone holding the bug holds a measurable edge over his foes. I know some lowball players who adhere to the practice of "no bug, no bet," though you're unlikely to find players that tight in a typical home game.

In *Kansas City lowball*, also known as *deuce-to-seven lowball*, the best low is not the standard 5-4-3-2-A, but rather 7-5-4-3-2. Aces count as high cards only, and straights and flushes also count as high hands. Either lowball version is perfectly kosher for your home game, but make sure everyone understands which version is being played. Foes could come to blows if one player is playing deuce-to-seven while his rival is playing *wheel low is best low.*

Razz is a hybrid of lowball and seven-card stud. It's structured like seven-stud, but the best low hand is the sole pot winner. *Wheel low is best low,* and straights and flushes don't count against you. I've heard of razz played Kansas City style, where the best low is deuce-to-seven, and straights and flushes do count against you. Either variation is fine, and there's no reason not to jazz things up with a little razz from time to time. However, make sure everyone is on the same wavelength when the deal commences or you'll have some very unhappy campers on your hands.

6

ODDS MADE EASY

♠

Some poker players are brilliant with numbers. They can quickly analyze any situation and spit out the odds of hitting a straight, flush, hanging curve, or decent nine-iron to the green. While I respect the innate ability of such math weenies, I know from long experience that higher math skills are not necessary for success in poker. There are some basic numbers you need to know, and some basic concepts you need to master, but beyond that . . . not so much. Knowing that your chance of drawing one card to an inside straight is *exactly* .0851063 is not demonstrably more useful than knowing you're about 10 to 1 against hitting. It may be less useful, in fact, if your analysis of the numbers goes so deep that it takes you out of the flow of the game. There is, in other words, such a thing as math overkill.

When we speak of odds in poker, we're usually speaking about the chances of an event *not* happening—*odds against*, in other words. If you're looking at a draw with 5–1 odds, for example, that's a draw you'll successfully complete only once, on average, for every five times you fail. The other way people talk about odds is in terms of the *odds offered* on a betting proposition. Someone who offers you 3–2 odds on a football game is promising to pay you three dollars for every two you bet, assuming that your team wins. When the odds against a certain outcome are identical to the odds-payoff if you win, the proposition is said to have *true odds*. The best example of this is that coin flip we considered earlier: Heads I win, tails you lose, and a dollar changes hands either way. It's a fifty-fifty proposition with a fifty-fifty payout, so it has true odds.

We spoke earlier of betting with the best of it. We can now nail down that concept by attaching to it the words *pot odds*. Pot odds are the odds offered by any given poker pot, i.e., the amount of money in the pot at the time you bet, measured against the amount you have to bet. If there's $4 in the pot and it costs you $1 to call, then your $1 bet stands to win you an additional $4; you're getting 4–1 pot odds. If you had to call a $2 bet in that same situation, you'd be getting only a 4 to 2 return on your investment, or pot odds of 2–1.

The only numbers you really need to know in poker, then, are a rough approximation of the pot odds, and a rough approximation of the *card odds*, the likelihood of any given poker outcome. With these two pieces of information, you can always know whether you're betting with the best of it or not. If the pot odds are bigger than the card odds, you're getting a positive return on your investment and you'll make money in the long run. If the pot odds are smaller than the card odds, you'll lose money in the long run.

Say you're playing draw poker and you're thinking of drawing one card to a flush, a hand you're pretty sure will be a winner if it hits. Your odds against completing the flush are about 4–1. In order to get to the draw, though, you have to call a bet. If you're calling a $1 bet into a $10 pot, that's 10–1 pot odds, plenty enough to justify your draw. But if it's a $1 bet into a $2 pot, your pot odds are only 2–1, and calling in this case would be a losing proposition.

Easy, right? Except that the heat of battle may not be the best time to stop and crunch all these numbers. For one thing, if you stop and go into a big think (with or without pencil and paper) every time you have a draw, your opponents will quickly figure out the kinds of hands you have at those times, and who wants to give away that kind of information? Also, in a home game setting, you may find that your friendly foes are less than patient about your detours down these mathematical byways. So here's the simple, simpler, simplest means of charting your course through the rocky shoals of pot odds versus card odds.

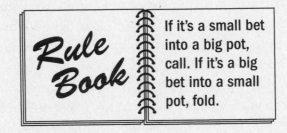

Rule Book

If it's a small bet into a big pot, call. If it's a big bet into a small pot, fold.

It's a rule of thumb, and we know that thumbs can sometimes get hammered, but it won't lead you too far astray because it will generally keep you from making expensive calls when the pot's not rich enough to reward you.

Sometimes people get tired of talking about odds, so they talk about *probability* instead. Probability, in a sense, expresses odds in reverse, telling you how *likely* an outcome is, where odds tell you how *unlikely* it is. Something with a 1 in 10 probability is identical to a thing with 9–1 odds against. You might describe this same event as "having one chance in ten," or a 10 percent shot. Probability, chance, and percentage all describe the same thing.

If you have trouble distinguishing between odds and probability, try this: Take the odds, add one number to the fat end, then flip the numbers over. This will yield the probability or chance. Example: Your odds of being dealt two suited cards as a starting hand in hold'em are 3–1 against. Add one to the three, making it four, reverse the order of the numbers and you have a 1 in 4 *probability* that your cards will be suited.

When we start to take a closer look at the numbers of poker, some sobering truths are revealed, and awareness of these truths can keep us out of all sorts of money-losing situations. Mostly the numbers remind us that long shots aren't called long shots for nothing, and that we should only chase them when the pot odds warrant. To put it another way, long shots need big pots. That's easy enough to remember, and if you have the discipline to stick to this wisdom, you'll find yourself betting with the best of it most of the time.

Here are some numbers you might find handy—if not now, then soon, after you've had a chance to integrate basic math with basic poker strategy. You might want to turn down the corners of these pages so you can refer back to them later as needed.

Five-card Poker (Draw or Stud)

You'll start with . . .	Roughly one time in . . .
Pair	1.5
Two pair	21
Trips	47

Straight	255
Flush	509
Full house	694
Quads	4,165
Straight flush	64,974

How rare is a straight flush? If you started playing draw poker on Christmas Day and played twenty-five hands an hour, nonstop around the clock, you'd be well into spring before the averages dictated that you're overdue to hit that hand.

Texas Hold'em

You'll start with . . .	Roughly one time in . . .
Suited cards	4
A pair or an ace	5
Unsuited cards 10 or higher	11
Any pair	17
Suited cards 10 or higher	33
Pair of jacks or higher	56
A–K unsuited	111
Pair of aces	221
A–K suited	332

We tend to underestimate the strength of our opponents' hands in hold'em, but think about this: In a ten-handed game, an average of two players on every deal will have hands containing an ace or a pair. This means that if you *don't* have one of those hands, you're starting out in third place at best.

Seven-Card Stud

You'll start with . . .	Roughly one time in . . .
Any pair	6
Three cards to a straight	6
Three suited cards	19
A pair of aces	77
Trips	425
Trip aces	5,525

Here's an odds oddity: If you have four cards to a flush, there are nine cards that complete your flush, compared to only eight that would complete an open-ended straight. Why, then, is a flush ranked higher than a straight when it's seemingly easier to hit? The answer lies in the fact that it's harder to *start out* with four cards to a flush than with four to an open-ended straight, and therefore overall harder to make that hand.

Here are some further numbers of note. You don't need all of these now. You might not need some of them ever. But if you ever find yourself wondering . . .

In Texas hold'em:
- The odds against flopping a flush are 118–1.
- The odds against flopping trips after starting with two un-paired cards are 73–1.
- The odds against flopping two pair to two unpaired cards are 48–1.
- The odds against flopping four to a flush after starting suited are 8–1.
- The odds against flopping three of a kind after starting with a pair are 7.5–1.

- The odds against flopping a pair to two unpaired cards are 3–1.

In hold'em on the turn and the river:
- The odds against completing a full house with two pair are 5–1.
- The odds against completing a full house with trips are 2–1.
- The odds against completing an inside straight draw are 5–1.
- The odds against completing an open-ended straight draw are 2–1.
- The odds against completing a four-card flush draw are 2–1.

In Omaha/8:
- If you start with A-2, you'll make your low one time in four.
- If you start with A-2-3, you'll make your low two times in three.
- If you start with A-2-3-4, you'll make your low one time in two.

In seven-card stud, if you stay for seven cards:
- The odds against turning trips into a full house or better are about 1.5–1.
- The odds against turning a pair into trips or better are about 4–1.
- The odds against turning a pair into two pair are about 1.5–1.
- The odds against turning three suited cards into a flush are about 4.5–1.

So what do you do with all these numbers, besides quail beneath the headache they cause? You might consider memorizing them, but the figures you memorize might not fit the situation you find yourself in. Alternatively, you can puzzle out the probabilities on the spot, but this will draw undue attention to the fact that you're the sort of player who bothers to figure the odds. For strategic reasons, you might not want to do this, since you'd probably like to present yourself as no better informed than any of your opponents.

Wouldn't it be handy to have a fast, easy shortcut for figuring out your chances of making the hand you need to make in any situation whatsoever?

I happen to have one here . . .

To calculate your chances on the fly, just count your *outs* (cards that will give you a winning hand), multiply them by the number of cards to come, and then multiply that number by 2 percent. A typical situation for this is after the flop in hold'em, when you have two more cards, the turn and the river, to come. If you've got 8 outs in this circumstance (as you would with an open-ended straight draw), then you multiply 8 by 2 for 16 and by 2 percent for 32 percent. This is not exactly the true probability of 33 percent, but it's "close enough for government work," close enough for you to know where you stand in the hand, and easy enough to calculate in an instant, especially after you've had some practice.

This trick works because there are 52 cards in a deck, roughly one half of one hundred. If there were exactly 50 cards in the deck, multiplying by 2 percent would always give you the precise probability. Those extra two cards skew the numbers, but not so much that the tool ceases to be useful. Suppose you have an inside straight draw in hold'em on the river. With four cards in your hand and four cards exposed, your chances of hitting are 4 out of 44, a true percentage of .09. Multiplying 4 outs times 1 times 2 percent yields a figure of .08. Either way, you can tell that you're a big underdog in this hand. At this point you can remind yourself that "long shots need big pots" and decide whether the size of the pot warrants your call.

Above all, don't get flustered by numbers. As you'll soon see, there are some sound basic strategies for poker that absolutely transcend the math of the game. If all you have is math in poker, you don't have enough to win, but if you don't have any math at all, you can probably still come out ahead.

7

BASIC POKER STRATEGY

♠

$\mathbf{R}$ight now I'd like to introduce you to some new ways of thinking about poker, ways to take your game to the next level. I have two goals here. One is to help you perform more successfully in the "small pond" of home poker. The other is to help prepare your eventual move into cardroom poker. Not all the "how to shred your home game" principles apply in the public poker setting, but many do, and the underlying mind-set—*I'm here to dominate and crush*—is always the same, no matter where the chips go in.

I've said that home poker should be fun, and it should be, but there's more than one definition of fun. Consider: The more focused on winning than on having fun you are, the better your poker performance will be. Your discipline and concentration will let you grab a greater share of pots and profit. You will, in other words, *win more*. And winning, I'm sure you'll agree, is more fun than losing. So we arrive at a conundrum that's almost Zenlike in its purity:

To have more fun, forget about fun.

Fun, in most home players' minds, equals *action*. If they're splashing around in the pot, they're having fun. If they're sitting there quietly, waiting for the next hand to start, they're *not* having fun. If *fun* equals *action*, and *action* is all that matters, they may find it literally impossible to throw away a hand. They'll justify their calls with sayings such as "Any two will do" or "Gots to see the flop," but the bottom line is they're playing too loose (where loose equals calling too much and staying too long with inferior hands). It's easy to see how this happens. Hell, I see it in myself every time I play. The cards are dealt . . . I pick up a crummy hand . . . I know I should throw it away . . . but these guys play so s-l-o-w. It'll be a good five minutes before I get another hand to look at, and what'll I do in the meantime? Eat more cold pizza? Not good for my waistline. Crack open a beer? Not good for my waistline *or* my performance. Read a book? Do a crossword puzzle? Be serious.

So maybe I'll just play this hand here. It'll keep me in action. It might even turn into a winner.

There you have it, the ultimate siren song of home poker: *It might even turn into a winner.* If you play every hand, you'll never be out of the action and you'll never miss out on a winner. As I said, most home poker players play too loose. Some play shockingly loose, and we like having them in our game because, though they occasionally get lucky (sometimes shockingly lucky), they generally donate. Look, let's not kid ourselves: These people are our friends, maybe even our close personal friends, but if they're going to *give* their money away, they might as well give it to us. And so we come to a fundamental rule of home poker:

Rule Book

If you have a bad hand, fold. Don't give more action than you get.

Don't play bad hands and don't make loose calls. Make your profit from those who do. If you have a bad hand, just fold. Find something useful to occupy your mind while you wait for the next hand to start.

Here's something useful: Ghost the other players. To *ghost* another player means to figure out what you think he has, correlate your guess with his actions, keep updating your guesses as the hand evolves, then watch at the showdown and see if you were right. Not only will this give you something to do between playable hands, it will actually improve your performance, because ghosting your foes must naturally and inevitably give you a better sense of what they consider to be good hands and shrewd moves. By watching the other players when you're not in the hand, you'll acquire much better *reads* on all of them, and even if you've been playing against the same seven guys for the last 128 consecutive Wednesdays, there's always room to improve your reads. Also, successfully ghosting your foes is fun. When you put a player on a hand, and that turns out to be the hand he has, you experience a sense of satisfaction as warm and fuzzy as the one that comes from dragging a pot. Well, almost.

How important is it not to play too loose? If you did nothing else but tighten up your starting requirements, you could beat most home games most of the time. The math of this is simple: Your net profit is the amount of chips you win, *minus the ones you give back*. Most players give back way too much with loose calls and reckless adventures. *If you just skip the give-back part of the party, you'll come out well ahead over time.*

You might run into a problem with this. You might get a reputation as a too-tight, "no fun" player. This rep probably wouldn't hurt your action in the long run because most home players, being too loose by nature, will give you plenty of play, even though they know you only make quality starts. It might, however, degrade the picture you want to create of yourself as just another loose, goofy gambler mixing it up on poker night. So now I'm going to give you a mechanism for shedding your too-loose image while, at the same time, dealing yourself a gigantic edge. It's just one word. Are you ready for it? Here it comes.

raise!

That's right, *raise*. When you get a weak hand, fold, but *when you get a strong hand, don't just call along . . . raise!* This will do many good things for you. First, it'll completely kill the idea that you're a tight player, because tight players (it is generally believed) do not raise. Second, it'll give you control of many betting situations because people generally defer to the active raiser. Third, in split-pot games it may put you in a situation of splendid isolation, where you're going solo for one half of the pot while two or more opponents duke it out in the other direction. Fourth, it will push certain other (timid) players outside their comfort range. It may even put them on tilt. Let's look at this and see how it happens.

Your basic Timid Timmy is both loose and weak. He calls too much and raises too little. He wants the most he can possibly get for the least he can possibly bet. Timmy wants to know he has a winning hand before he starts committing a lot of chips, and so has a strong interest in *cheap flops* (flops he can see for a single bet). He's comfortable with the stakes he plays at, but when you start raising a lot, you arbitrarily double those stakes. Now that $1 flop is routinely costing $2. He won't stop calling—he didn't come here to fold—he'll just end up paying a higher price for the basic mistake he's making by calling too much in the first place.

He may become annoyed. He may accuse you of spoiling his fun, and he may even try to slow you down: "Do you have to raise *every* hand? Your cards can't be that good *all* the time." At this point you might claim to have a disease—*raisitis*—which makes you make raises against your will. In fact, you're being selective about your raises, but Timmy doesn't know that. He just thinks you're out of line and trying to push him around.

Well, he's not going to let himself get bullied, no sir! He'll raise you right back! Or no, not raise, because, remember, he's timid. But he'll *call*, all right! He'll call in the most forthright, aggressive manner imaginable.

With his weak hand and his crumbling attitude.

Whose chances do you like right now?

Me, I like yours.

Are you cruel to treat Timmy this way? Are you deriving unseemly satisfaction from pushing around a putative friend? This is poker, folks. Each of us is responsible for our own good time. Timmy gets his by playing many, many hands and counting on luck to lead him to the promised land. You get yours by playing excellent poker, by pitting your skills and awareness (and aggres-siveness and bully behavior) against the other guys at the table. If they beat you, so be it, but the one thing you want to do is *always play your best*. And strong play generally equals best play.

So we have the start of a poker philosophy.

Rule Book

Play fewer hands than everyone else, but when you do play, play powerfully.

This is called *selective-aggressive* poker, and it's a sound formula for success in most home games. Trouble is, if you follow this path, it won't take long for even your least observant opponents to see that you're *not one of them*. But you want them to think that you *are* one of them, no more skilled or focused than they are, and not concerned with anything but having a terrific time on poker night. Now we come to another big word, writ small:

image

Image is the picture of yourself you present to the other play-ers. There are all kinds of images you could choose to project. You might seem friendly or crazy or clueless or hopeless or lucky or hopelessly lucky. One thing these images have in common is: *They're all a big fat lie!* If you're a tricky, knowledgeable poker player, you want to come across as transparent and unschooled. If you're dangerous, you want to be disarming. If you're fearful, try to appear fearless. The whole goal of image play is to get your opponents to see you as you're not, and to make their decisions based on this misperception. To take an obvious example, if they think you're loose, they'll be loose, too.

Now, the fact is that many home poker players (and many, many players in cardrooms) don't pay any attention to the other players at the table. They make their betting decisions based on their hand, their whole hand, and nothing but their hand, so help them God. Nevertheless, impressions do build up over time, and if you have the impression of being a heartless bastard in your home game, concerned with nothing but squeezing the last dime from your near and dear, there's a very good chance they'll stop inviting you to play.

It happened in my home game, to this fellow named Ross. Ross was a good player—terrific—but we never begrudged him that. After all, we all thought we were pretty terrific, too. No, Ross's problem was his attitude. He attacked everyone with savage glee, demeaned the play of others, and never stopped crowing about how smart he was, how much he won, how effortlessly he outwitted us all. He was a buzz kill, plain and simple, and singularly out of step with the game. So we got together and decided that "Ross must be tossed." Since then, it has become part of our vocabulary, the microculture of our game: *You better stay in line*, goes the (mocking) threat, *or you might get Rossed*.

To avoid getting Rossed from a home game, simply throw a little image into the mix. Tell some jokes. Maybe don't raise *all* the time. Talk about how badly you play. Call attention to mistakes you make (even if they're not really mistakes). Above all, if you think you're better than they are, never let them know. Paradoxically, one way to achieve this deception is simply to tell them you think you're better. They'll never believe you and will conclude that you live in a soft pink (and highly exploitable) cloud of arrogant self-delusion.

This might be a good time to trot out another important poker rule, one which speaks to the nature of truth and lies in poker.

Rule Book

Deception is what you do to others—delusion is what you do to yourself. Project your Image, but don't fall for it.

It's fine to project the impression of looseness or recklessness, but if you use image play as an excuse to play badly, you're just defeating your own purpose. Think of yourself as a radio station: You're broadcasting a certain signal, but the in-studio monitors are set to "mute."

Which image is best for you? You'll have to try a few to know, and not everyone can sell every image. Some players can project *scary*, but they can't sell *clueless*. Some can act *loose* while playing *tight*, but for others, the only way to seem loose is to *be* loose, and as we've already discussed, that's no good. Your best image is one that comes from your essential nature. I can sell *playful* with no problem, because I'm a pretty playful guy to begin with. I have trouble (I'm not sorry to say) acting persuasively like an asshole, though I know many players for whom projecting the asshole image is an absolute strength of their game.

Is it possible to project an image against people you play with regularly? Sure it is. Everyone has good days and bad days, and everyone has moods. If you arrive at the game bitching about the traffic or your boss or your upset stomach, everyone will figure that, tonight at least, you seem to be off your game. They'll interpret your ultra-aggressive play as a function of your anger or your upset stomach. Yes, it's an acting job, but not a terribly taxing one, and it's fundamental to your success in poker.

As an added benefit, the minute you start to concern yourself with such things as image, you take your game to different, better place. Now instead of thinking only about what cards you hold, you're addressing the question of what cards they *think* you hold. You'll also become more aware of the images that your foes are trying to sell (even if they're not aware of it themselves). You will become adept at seeing through smoke screens and detecting the real nature of the players you face. This will help you expand your expertise into the two areas we'll address next: *bluffing* and *tells*.

♦ ♦ ♦ Bluffing

Conventional wisdom says that it's not possible to bluff in most low-limit poker games (which most home games are) for the simple reason that most players aren't paying enough attention to be bluffed. If they like their hand, they'll call no matter what—and with no thought to you. This is true to a certain extent, but to my way of thinking, conventional wisdom is for conventional people; we need to look beyond.

Certain bluffs *never* work, nor should they. If the pot is large enough, and there's any reasonable chance that your opponent is bluffing, you should probably call most of the time, even if most of the time you lose. Let me give you an extreme example to illustrate the point.

Suppose you and Vlad the Impaler are the last two players in the pot. Even though you're playing $1–2 limit, the pot has grown to the stratospheric sum of $300 (I told you it was an extreme example). On the last round of betting, Vlad bets. You know Vlad. You've played against him for years, and you almost never see him bluff. In fact, right now you're 99 percent sure that he's not bluffing. But there's $300 in the pot, and it only costs you $2 to call. If he's not bluffing, you lose $2, but if he *is* bluffing, you win $300. That's a 150–1 return on your investment. Since you figure that there's only a 1 in 100 chance Vlad is bluffing, you'll lose $2 every 99 times you make this call, for a total loss of $198. But that 1 time out of 100 that he *is* bluffing, you'll win $300. Your net gain over time is $102. It's right to call, then, when your pot odds (potential payouts) are greater than the odds against your being wrong.

In practical terms, the pots aren't usually so overwhelmingly large, so the logic of calling isn't so clear. Most people don't care about that, though. They look at all those chips in the middle of the table and figure, *What the hell.* They'll throw in that last bet "just for the size of the pot" or "just to keep you honest" or "just to see what you've got." Or maybe they're getting all macho: "Damned if I'll surrender without a fight." It's a sad thing when you've done everything in your power to convince a foe to fold, but he decides to waste a final bet anyhow. Can't you teach these people *anything*?

In home games, then, it's hard to bluff on the final round of betting because most home players, being too loose, will call you more than they should. That's okay. That just means that they'll call you too often with worse hands, and you'll make your money that way. But it *doesn't* mean you should never try to bluff. You just have to pick your spots.

Suppose you're playing a game like seven-card stud, high-low split, chip declare, no qualifier. Looking around the board, you see a lot of high door cards, and only one or two low door cards, with your deuce being the lowest of all. Of course it helps if your hole cards are low, but you're in a perfect position to *drive a bluff* regardless. Simply bet as if you have a strong low hand. Your foes have seen you do this often enough. They know that you like to play your good low hands fast. They also know that once you start betting, you're not likely to stop. Maybe they'll decide to get out of your way early. Maybe not, but as long as you keep getting low upcards, you'll keep betting and raising, and keep giving them a chance to fold. If your upcards continue to be good, you'll have a *scary board* (a hand that appears strong) to help you sell your bluff, leaving you (you hope) as the only player left declaring low at the end and earning you half the pot without a showdown.

You might be tempted to show your bluff to show how clever you are. Don't do it. That's just boastful, and counterproductive. If you're going to boast, boast *and* lie. Boast about what great cards you've been getting. Boast about how you were a lock to win the hand from the start. Maybe they won't believe you, but since you don't have to show your hand, they'll never know—and you'll reinforce your image as someone who only bets with the best of it.

Sometimes the cards don't come your way, and you have to *break off a bluff*. Let's say you start with that same deuce door card and bet big on the first round. On the next card, though, you pick up an unhelpful card like a jack. Can you continue to drive at the pot? No. Your board's not scary enough. Betting big now would just be a waste of money. Fold if anyone bets, and don't forget to lament about how you keep getting bricked out after strong starts. This will make your bluffs that much more convincing when you do get help from cooperative cards.

Put your bluffs in context. Adjust your actions to fit the situation, your image, and the other players' states of mind. Your foes are playing *hands*, but you're playing *a game*. Can you see the distinction? You're in this for the long haul. If the cards don't happen to cooperate this time or the next time, who cares? Remember, everyone gets their fair share of luck; it's your skill and your awareness that will make you a money winner over time.

Time for another rule from the rule book, although this is more like a philosophy than a rule. Yet it may help you keep your head on straight when things are temporarily not going your way.

Rule Book

You're born broke, you die broke—everything else is just fluctuation.

I want to stress this point: You're going to be playing poker *for the rest of your life!* What happens tonight in terms of dollars won and dollars lost just couldn't matter less. The only thing that matters is making quality decisions: bringing your best game to the table every time you play. *Play right now.* That's the goal you want to serve.

There's nothing more sublime than stealing a pot with a naked bluff—talk about *fun!* In that moment you realize that you've gone beyond cards, you've gone beyond luck. You've become a *player*. Inevitably, though, there are times when you'll get caught stealing. Don't hang your head. Some players would. Some players, you know, never bluff because they can't stand the (perceived) humiliation of getting caught. They don't realize that getting caught is not a problem, it's an opportunity. The moment you're caught bluffing, your image shifts from tight to loose, from straightforward to tricky. For the next few hands, maybe the next many hands, your opponents will view all your actions with a jaundiced eye. They'll call you *a lot* because now they know what a Bluffy Blufferson you are. Your response? Adjust. Screw down your starting requirements. Play only premium hands, but *push them hard*. Give yourself that precious head start we've been talking about. They'll call because they don't believe you, and they'll lose because this time you're telling the truth. Eventually they'll get tired of losing to your superior hands. They'll start folding more often. Now your image has swung back from loose to tight and you can resume your thieving ways.

Bluffing, in sum, is the art of getting them leaning the wrong way. The thing to keep in mind is that they're *always* leaning some way. No one's judgment is perfect. If you can just see yourself as others see you, you'll know what they expect of you, and you'll know how to best them with their own flawed perception. As Wee Willie Keeler used to say, "Hit 'em where they ain't."

Some players try to bluff but fail because they give too much away. You've seen it before: Someone calls someone down and says, "I knew it! I *knew* you were bluffing." How did he know? Something told him. Something called, appropriately enough, a *tell*.

♦ ♦ ♦ Tells

Tells are betrayals—unconscious or habitual acts or actions, or even sounds or words that indicate to your opponents how you feel about your hand and what you intend to do. Suppose you're pre-flop in a hand of hold'em, and you're trying to decide whether to try stealing the pot with a raise. Looking *downstream* (at the players who will act after you), you notice that Astro Boy has a look of disgust on his face, Felix is sighing, and Wilma is ready to toss her cards in the muck. These are tells, folks. They tell you that the players behind you have lost interest in their hands. This information gives you much more freedom to get frisky with the pot. The field has thinned itself, with no real help from you.

Or maybe you're playing high-low seven-card stud and you're thinking you might be able to steal the low. You're not sure, though, and Stumpy in particular has you stumped, because his hand looks like it could go either way, with board cards of A♥-8♥-5♥ as the sixth street cards come out. Now Stumpy gets a K♥. His eyes go wide. He sits up straight in his chair. His nostrils flare. Does he like that card? What do you think? Now that you know Stumpy is drawing to the flush (has made it, more likely), you can go after the low without fear of competition.

Maybe you're second to act. Sid has bet and you're unsure about whether to call. Glancing downstream, you see Nancy reaching for her chips, and not just to call but to raise. Sid, meanwhile, has this light in his eye that tells you if Nancy raises, Sid will be only happy to reraise, and you'll be stuck for three bets—four if Nancy raises him back. Well, your hand might be good for one bet, but it's sure not good for four. You fold, silently thanking Sid and Nancy for making your path so clear.

Not all tells are this obvious, of course. Poker would be almost too easy if they were. But there are plenty of tells out there if you know what to look for and how to spot them. You begin to build up a library of reliable indicators, particularly when you play against the same people week after week or month after month. Boris lights his cigar when he's lost interest in the hand. Rocky mutters, "I crawl" when he calls on a draw. Natasha bets out of turn when she's strong.

Tell-hunting can be as rewarding and fulfilling as ghosting your foes. There's delight in the discovery, for instance, that Wilbur's horse laugh is a dead-certain giveaway that he's missed his draw, for he never makes a sound when he hits. Even the way a player announces his actions can be a tell. When Fidel has a powerful hand, his chin drops to his chest and he barely whispers, "Raise," as if he's hoping to slip his bet into the pot unnoticed. His very attempt to disguise his strength reveals it. As Mike Caro pointed out in his groundbreaking *Mike Caro's Book of Poker Tells*, unsophisticated players who are strong will reliably act weak, and those who are weak will reliably act strong. Using these *reverse tells* or *false tells*, they try to manipulate you with inaccurate information. Often, as in Fidel's case, they just end up transmitting a code that's astoundingly easy to break. Against opponents tricky enough to use deception but not tricky enough to use it well, simply ask yourself what response (call or fold) your foe is trying to induce, and then do the opposite.

Of course there's such a thing as a *double-reverse tell*, like acting strong when you *are* strong, in hopes that the action will be seen as deliberate, though clumsy, deception, and you'll get the call you're after. Whether your opponents are given to true tells or fake tells or fake true tells will depend on their level of sophistication and caginess. Whatever their level, though, it's not likely to change, especially in home games where people don't think they need to adjust (or even monitor) their behavior in order to win.

Do you give off tells? Probably. If you don't now, you have before. Everybody does when they're first starting out, either because they're not aware of the concept or because, like poor Fidel, they think they're being terribly tricky. Early in my playing days I consistently (and unwittingly) committed a particular tell: a *pro-tect-my-cards tell*. I'd look at my hand, and if I liked it, I'd lay it down on the table with some chips on top of it to protect it from being accidentally swept into the muck or otherwise fouled. If I didn't like it, I wouldn't protect it. What was the point, since I'd soon be folding anyhow? Savvy opponents could tell at a glance how I felt about my cards. One day my wife noticed my tell and called it to my attention. If she hadn't alerted me, and if I hadn't been willing to listen, I might still be giving myself away.

There's a certain lesson in humility in this. We like to think that we're smart enough and self-aware enough not to give off obvious tells. When our tells (or indeed any of our flaws) are pointed out to us, we tend to get defensive. We become more concerned with protecting our fragile egos than with improving our play. Superior players learn to leave their egos out of it, and this is a model we all should follow. You'll never be able to erase your tells if you can't spot them, sure, but also if you deny they're there. Have a trusted friend watch you play, and ask him to point out your tells. You'll profit from what he says, provided you're brave enough to listen.

You'll also do well to watch yourself as if you were watching another player and see if you can pick off your own tells. In a quiet moment you could even draw up a list of them. The mere act of writing down your weaknesses in this area will help you eliminate them. Regarding your opponents' ability to spot your tells, recognize that your foes fall into two categories: those who look for tells and those who don't. The fact is that some players are so wrapped up in looking at and thinking about their own cards that they are simply blind to the wealth of available information other players might provide. Don't *you* be blind. Make it a habit to watch the other players. Their body language, their unintended tics and flinches, will tell you a lot.

Unless they're lying, of course. Intelligent players can effectively mask their reactions—but other intelligent players can often see behind those masks. Don't attempt reverse tells against good players unless you're confident you can pull them off, for what you imagine to be deceptive may, like Fidel's chin on his chest, be blatantly obvious. Some of your opponents will be particularly good at picking off tells. They can detect your intention just by looking in your eyes. Don't get into staring contests with them. Just look away. Look away when you're bluffing and look away when you're strong. Don't try to send misleading messages. Superior foes will decipher them, and even weaker opponents will intuit patterns over time. Behave neutrally and consistently. They can't go to school on your actions if you always act the same.

If you feel like your eyes say too much, you can always wear sunglasses or a hat with the brim pulled down low—but that won't do you much good if your slumping shoulders give you away. I always wear a baseball cap when I play poker. I just feel more comfortable knowing I can conceal my face in shadow if I choose. (I don't wear sunglasses, though. Sure, they can't see my eyes—but I can't see the cards!) The best thing we can do in this area is to work on our *poker face*, our ability to betray nothing, no matter how the cards come down. We achieve this ability by seeing ourselves as others see us and then by being honest enough to see ourselves as we really are.

Poker and ego are all wrapped up in one another. Just as ego prevents us from admitting our tells or other flaws, it may also tempt us to tell others what we've spotted in them. You might want to point out someone's tells, or indeed any of his mistakes, just to show how smart you are. Resist that urge! A reliable tell is worth much more than good cards or lucky draws. Keep your knowledge to yourself. The Enigma team at Bletchley Park would hardly have served the Allied cause by boasting to the Nazis that they'd broken their code. When you're at the poker table, you're at war. Loose lips sink ships.

So now you have a basic recipe for success in poker: tight, aggressive play supported by image management, abetted by keen awareness, and not betrayed by tells or ego. There's much more to say on the subject of poker strategy, so let's get to it, breaking it down game by game as we go.

8

HOLD'EM BATTLE PLAN

♠

In this chapter we'll discuss starting requirements and other tactical considerations for the game of Texas hold'em. These pages will only scratch the surface of strategic hold'em thinking, but they'll be enough to get you started, and to allow you to feel confident about the decisions you make when you play. Later, when you've got these basics under your belt, you can continue with other books, simulation software, and so on. One thing you'll learn is that learning never stops. In fact, the worst thing a poker player can do is imagine that he ever knows it all. When that happens, complacency and arrogance set in, opening the door to sloppy, lazy play. What's that thing that pride goeth before? Oh, yeah. A fall.

A student of poker is a student forever. If you play against the same people week after week, eventually they *will* figure you out. To keep winning, you must keep growing and changing. If you're diligent, you'll always be a step or two ahead and you can continue to pick their pockets not with glee or with greed but with the deep satisfaction of a job well done. And when you venture beyond your home game into the wide world of public poker, you'll certainly want to go there armed. Here, then, are your guns and ammo.

The first critical question you face in hold'em—or indeed in any poker game—is: "Which hands should I play?" What's a quality starting hand and what's an automatic fold? The answer often depends on the tenor of the game you're in. Is it tight or loose? Are you likely to face many raises? Will people pay you off with holdings worse than yours? In hold'em in general, though, the rule of thumb is *the higher, the better.* Let's take a closer look.

Starting hands in hold'em can be divided into six categories: pairs, suited cards, connected cards, suited connectors, high cards, and ragged hands or *rags.*

Pairs have value because they don't necessarily need to improve to win. If you take a pair of aces, for example, up against a pair of threes, you'll win every time that a three doesn't come on the board, and you'll still win if a three comes but an ace comes, too. Obviously you don't want to be on the other end of this equation, holding the lower pair and chasing upstairs into a bigger pair. That's why *high pairs are the best hands in hold'em.* They dominate low pairs (and unpaired hands) and can win without help.

Suited hands are those with two cards in the same suit. Start with suited cards and you only need three cards of your suit on-board to make a flush—but you do need those cards. Unlike pairs, suited cards can't win without help from the board. That's why we call them *drawing hands.* High suited cards are better than low suited cards because if a flush does come, the winner will be the player with the highest top card. If you start with A♥-T♥ and I have Q♥-J♥, I'm better off not hitting my flush. A flush facing a bigger flush is a pricey proposition!

Connected cards are drawing hands where the cards are not suited but adjacent to one another in rank, hands like K-Q, T-9 or 6-5. As with flush draws, you'll need to improve to win. If you have a hand like 9-8, for instance, and the flop comes T-7-2, you've got an open-ended straight draw. If a J or 6 comes on the turn or the river, you have a big hand. Otherwise . . . *bupkes*. As with flushes, you want to avoid having a smaller straight than your foe. Sad you will be if you hold 7-6 when the board shows T-9-8 and your opponent has Q-J.

Suited connectors, hands like K♥-Q♥ and 8♦-7♦, are attractive hands because they can improve either to straights or flushes. Obviously they could also improve to pairs, two pairs, trips, or full houses, but in any case they do have to improve. If you're holding something like J♠-T♠ and the flop comes 9♠-8♦-2♠, you're said to have a *big draw*, because any queen or seven will give you a straight, any spade completes your flush, and any jack or ten gives you top pair on board. Here again, you'd like high cards better than low ones. In fact, low suited connectors, hands like 4♣-5♣, are such losers that they go by the fond sobriquet *stupid connectors*.

Unpaired, unconnected, unsuited high card hands can coordinate with the board to create high pairs or two-pair holdings or, much less frequently, top straights. Every now and then, they'll make a flush when the board comes with four of one of their suits, but that's such a long shot as to be beyond your rational consideration when weighing the strength of your hand. A hand like K-Jo (o=offsuit) or Q-To looks rather pretty but, as with any suited or connected hand, you'll have to hit to win.

Rags are holdings like K-8, J-2, 6-4, 8-5—basically any hand that's not high or suited or connected. These hands are automatic folds. Sometimes they'll seem playable, especially if they're suited, like K♦-2♦ or *one-gappers* like 9-7, but they're losing propositions, and the more often you fold them, the better off you'll be.

Even with your playable hands, you have to be aware of common pitfalls such as *kicker trouble*, where you have the same pair as another player, but a weaker kicker. Suppose you're holding A♦-K♠ and I have A♣-T♥. I like the look of my hand: That's two high cards, and I've been told that high cards are good in hold'em. But can you guess how often you'll beat me, thanks to your better kicker? Better than 70 percent of the time. Worse yet, I might not even know I'm in trouble. If I'm looking at a board of A-6-9-3-3, I might figure that I'm sitting pretty with aces and threes and a ten kicker. You, meanwhile, are lying in the weeds with your king kicker, just waiting to kick my . . . well, kick the sort of body part a kicker kicks.

It's easy to lose your discipline in hold'em. Once you've thrown away 8-5o, only to see the flop come 8-8-5, you'll start to believe in the seductive logic of "any two will do." While it's true that you might hit a big flop with any starting hands (heck, you only need three of a kind on board to make quads!), remember the horse race. You don't want to be in there when the other fellow has that big head start.

To maintain your hold'em rigor, simply ask yourself how much help you need from the flop in order to feel good about your hand. The more help you need, the less likely you should be to play. If you're holding 9-6, for example, just catching one nine or one six isn't going to brighten your day all that much. You really need to "hit the flop twice"—have two out of the three flop cards help your hand—in order to feel secure. Trouble is, you're not likely to hit the flop twice. Boards like 9-9-3 or 6-6-K or 6-9-2 put you in pretty good shape, but they're few and far between. You can dream, I suppose, of flopping T-8-7 or 8-7-5 for a straight, but that will happen less than once every 150 times you hold 9-6— and at that you might fall victim to someone holding, or drawing to, a higher straight.

Success in hold'em requires that you be disciplined and highly selective about the hands you decide to play, but this does not mean that undisciplined, undiscerning players never win. To the contrary! If you play hold'em for any length of time, you'll soon become familiar with the concept of the *bad beat* or *suckout*, wherein some knucklehead with inferior cards chases and chases and chases against long odds . . . and gets there.

Suppose you start with that powerhouse, A-A. You're a big favorite, so you raise, and you don't much mind when your pal Hermie calls along. He's loose, way too loose, and you know it. If he's got something like 7-6 offsuit (which we'll say is the case here), your aces will win more than four times out of five. This particular time the flop comes A-8-2. You've got a set of aces and he's got . . . *nada*. How big an underdog is he now? He'll win less than 5 percent of the time! But Hermie, God love him, doesn't know that, or doesn't care, and he calls your bet. The turn card is a 4, giving Hermie an inside straight draw. Hermie's grandmother never taught him not to draw to an inside straight, so now he's married to the pot, with no possibility of divorce. He only needs a 5 to beat you—and lo and behold, he hits his 10–1 shot on the river and cackles with glee as he rakes the pot.

Not very nice, Hermie . . . and you're sorely tempted to tell him what a numbskull he was for taking that draw in the first place. Let it go. Hermie made a big mistake, and got very lucky. It happens . . . not often . . . but confirmation bias, the tendency to remember unusual outcomes, will tell Hermie that it happens much more often than it does. The last thing you want to do is wise him up. After all, he is your friend, and he's entitled to play the game any way he chooses, especially when his choices are so long-term profitable for you. However, you might not be thinking long-term right now. You might be thinking short-term and, here in the short term, feeling stung. You might want to sting back. For the sake of easing your immediate psychic pain, you might want to excoriate Hermie for his terrible, terrible call. That might make you feel better; however, your goal here is not to feel good but to win money. Common courtesy and poker self-interest alike demand that you not deride Hermie for his errors, no matter how victimized those errors seem to make you feel.

In hold'em—in any form of poker—you need to learn to take your bad beats in stride. They'll happen. They must happen, because if they didn't happen, then the Hermies of this world would never be rewarded for their ridiculous draws. They'd go broke or get bored, and we'd all have to find something else to do with our time. In the cynical dialect of poker we are advised: "Don't tap on the glass." Let the fish swim around the tank as they see fit.

In poker, as we've already noted, information is power, and the later in the hand you act the more information you have to work with. For this reason, hold'em hands that are unplayable in early position, when information is scarce, are sometimes good for a call or even a raise in late position, when more is known about your opponents' relative strength. Suppose you're holding a hand like Q♣-J♣: high cards, suited and connected. It looks like a good hand—and maybe it is. But how many better hands are out there? If you call in early position, you're vulnerable to raises from anyone behind you with a big pair or a *good ace*, an ace with a good kicker, say A-K, A-Q, or A-J. But hold that same Q♣-J♣ in last position, when no one else has entered the pot and you face only the blinds, and now you can call or even raise, hoping that the blinds will fold, winning you the pot right there.

There are voluminous *start charts* that list which hold'em hands can be played in which position. You can find them in many poker books and liberally strewn across poker sites on the internet, and part of your ongoing poker education will be to investigate start charts and integrate their wisdom into your play. For now, how about a more minimalist start chart, based on the precept that hold'em is a game of *good cards* and *good position?*

JV's Reductio ad Absurdum Start Chart

---

good cards + good position = usually playable
good cards + bad position = sometimes playable
bad cards + good position = rarely playable
bad cards + bad position = never playable

This chart is not so much a guideline as it is a coaching device, designed to train you off the habit of getting involved in hold'em hands with inferior cards, especially inferior cards in bad position. You might not believe me now, if you have little experience with hold'em, but starting with good cards in good position is the single biggest leg up you can give yourself in this game.

After the flop, your magic words are *fit or fold*. That is, if the board cards don't coordinate with your cards, get out of the hand. It's a hole in many hold'em players' games that they continue to chase after the flop, even though they have no realistic prospect of winning the pot. Stay out of that hole and you'll save yourself many, many bets.

Here's a typical fit or fold situation.

Sanguine Cyril holds K♦-J♦. Waiting for the flop, he's thinking, *diamonds are a Cyril's best friend*. Alas, the flop comes 9♣-7♣-4♦. He has no pairs, and no realistic draws. He has whiffed, missed the flop completely. If there's any betting at all, Cyril must fold. But he's a hopeful guy, so he starts counting up his outs. He knows that there are three kings and three jacks in the deck, and allows himself to believe that any one of those six cards will give him the best hand. But is this true? The K♣ or J♣ complete a flush draw and the offsuit jacks complete a T-8 open-ended straight draw. This leaves just two kings as clean outs, cards that help him and probably no one else—no one, that is, except anyone with A-K or K-Q or, God forbid, K-K. But Cyril is not stayed. He now leads himself further astray by dreaming of catching two perfect cards in a row, a so-called runner-runner draw to his flush or straight. It's not impossible. Stranger things have happened. He'd just better hope that no one is out there with, say, the A♦-9♦, or Q-Jo, and drawing to a bigger flush or straight than him.

Why is Cyril in such trouble? Because he's filtering information through optimism, not realism. The fact is, he missed the flop. The other fact is, he *wishes* he hadn't. The *other* other fact is, his wishes trump his common sense and lead him to believe that he has a reasonable reason to call. Don't fall into Cyril's trap. When the flop comes, do a quick analysis of your prospects for improvement and measure those chances against the hands your opponents might hold. If you're in good shape, stick around. If you're not, admit that you're beaten and scram.

There are relevant numbers to back this up. You'll find them back in chapter six, but you don't need big math to know where you're at in hold'em. Mostly all you need is clarity of vision and the capacity to get away from your hand when your head tells you that you must. Most home game players, Action Jacksons that they are, lack both these skills, and once again you have the chance to set yourself apart just by avoiding the common mistakes that your regular opponents commonly make.

Rule Book

Fit or Fold.
Don't chase.

By the time the turn card comes, hands are fairly well defined. You've seen every card but one, and you know pretty much where you're at. Even the most dedicated dreamer, for example, knows he can no longer hope for a flush if there aren't enough suited cards out there for him to pin his dreams upon. In fixed-limit hold'em, the bet size is doubled on the turn, and this has an impact on people's thinking as well. A lot of players who will chase for a cheap card on the flop will give up their hand on the turn. This is very important information for a player like you, who has restricted his involvement to quality hands and only stuck around on the flop with promising prospects. In the best of circumstances, you have the best hand on the turn and your opponents have only hopes and dreams. Your job at this point is simple: *Bet. Make them pay or make them fold!*

Since the bet has doubled, though, you may be a little leery of betting the turn. Many novice hold'em players are. They look at the size of the pot and decide that it's big enough for them. If they're going to get drawn out on, they reason, they'd just as soon not lose any more money. This is disastrous thinking, and it's a function of playing *not to lose*, not playing to *win*. A timid player, playing not to lose, might check on the turn and give his opponents with slim draws a free card. He'll be plenty sorry if they improve enough to beat him, especially if he could have taken the pot by betting out on the turn. In the name of playing to win, therefore, go ahead and bet. This does several good things. First, it gives your opponents an opportunity to fold, which could win you the pot right there. Second, it gives them the chance to make a mistake, to take a draw that's a money-loser or chase you with an inferior hand. Third, and perhaps most important, it establishes you as a force to be reckoned with, a player who's not afraid to step up on the turn. Your fearlessness makes them fear you.

In many home games, these bets may be meaningless. Maybe your foes don't care about the money. Maybe they think you're just bluffing or being a bully (and as we've already discussed, they'll have none of *that*). Really, what you're doing is just following a basic precept of hold'em:

Rule Book

When you get the goods, bet the goods.

You made a considered decision to play this hand in the first place. You found a fit on the flop (or you'd have folded). Now you find yourself swallowing hard and firing aw°ay at the turn because you think you have the best hand. Your too-loose opponents will give you action here, and that's fine. Sometimes they'll draw out on you *and that's fine, too*. It'll keep them coming back for more.

♦ ♦ ♦ Tilt

If you do get drawn out on, you run the risk of going on *tilt*. Tilt is a phenomenon of poker where anger, or tiredness, or drunkenness, or a host of other "nesses," keep you from playing your best. Mostly it comes with a feeling of entitlement. You bet with the best of it. You were *entitled* to win. But you didn't win because the dim bulbs you play with insist on playing such crappy cards. *Well,* you might now find yourself thinking, *they're not the only ones who can win with bad cards!* Next thing you know, you're calling with junk and you're right down there in the mire with everyone else, playing a version of hold'em I call *hit to win*, where no one is playing strategically, or even sensibly, and the one who wins will merely be the one who hits his hand.

I hope you see that there's more to discipline than just starting with the right cards or folding if the flop doesn't fit. There's also mental rigor, your commitment to keep playing your best, no matter what. Especially in a home game, where players may not know about or care about the odds, and where the price of tilt may be relatively low (because other players are tilty too), it takes a certain . . . well, let's call it stubbornness . . . to keep yourself on course.

Some players on tilt will just go nuts, get out ahead of themselves on hand after hand, and get slaughtered as a result. For others, tilt is a descent into pessimism, into soft, weak, reactive poker. A player in this brand of funk will know he should be making strong turn bets, but he can't bring himself to pull the trigger. Feeling snakebit, he just *knows* they're going to call and just *knows* they're going to catch lucky. Hey, they might always call, but they won't always catch lucky. Remember the cardinal rule: *When you get the goods, bet the goods*. That's the secret to success on the turn.

On the river, when the cards are out and the pot is big, everyone's decisions get a lot easier to make. Either you've made your hand or you haven't. Either you have a winner or you don't. Either you think he's bluffing or he's not. They don't call it the showdown for nothing. Hold'em on the river is as binary as a gunfight. Somebody lives. Somebody dies. Next case.

The big difference between river play in home games and in clubs is that out there in public, people will often fold in the face of river bets. After all, everyone in a cardroom has made the decision to test his skills against strangers, and they're probably trying to play correctly. Whether they can actually do this or not remains to be seen, but you'll see at least some players who can make a *good laydown*, folding their hands when they know it's hopeless to call. In home games, where players are just frisking around, and "calling to keep them honest," it's much more difficult to win without a showdown. Moral of the story? *If you're playing hold'em at home, you'll probably have to show the best hand to win the pot.*

Does this mean that you must fold, must make that good laydown, when someone bets out on the river? Not necessarily. The unschooled home player who doesn't know enough to fold on the river probably also doesn't know enough not to bet into a better hand. Here's where you need to know your opponents. Does Bubba bluff? Will he press second-best hands or only bet with the nuts? Does he even know what the nuts are? If you've been ghosting your foes, you'll be well inside their heads by now, and have the information you need to make a sensible decision here.

Sensible decisions are not always easy to make. You might know you're beaten—just know it down there in the core of your being—and still not be able to get away from your hand. For many players it's a matter of machismo. Their pride won't allow them to be driven off a pot. The good news is they're never bluffed out. The bad news is they lose *a lot*. Don't fall prey to that flawed thinking. Acknowledge that you might be filtering your perception through hope or desire or longing. *See things as they are. If you're beaten, fold.* Use the money you saved by not calling to reward yourself with a frozen yogurt later.

♦ ♦ ♦ Watch the Showdown

Many players lose interest in the hand once they fold, especially if they fold on the river and would just as soon not watch "their" chips getting pushed to someone else. They turn their attention elsewhere and drift off into a fuzzy netherworld of nonconsciousness while they wait for the next hand to start. Big mistake! By ignoring the showdown, they're missing out on an unparalleled fact-finding opportunity. *When players turn over their cards at hand's end, they're offering you intimate insight into how they play the game.* It's there for you for free, if only you care to look.

Big Bob raises before the flop, and bets out again when the flop comes:

Nor does he slow down on the turn, when the 2♦ pairs the board. The river is an A♦, and Bob bets again. When he's called, he turns over a hand of . . . J♣-T♣, losing the pot to someone holding pocket nines.

Wow! What have we learned? That Bob will raise pre-flop with second-tier holdings like J-T suited. That he'll bet on the come with a decent draw. That he'll keep betting on the turn, even if the draw doesn't get there. That he'll essay a hopeless bluff on the river, when the only hands that can call him can beat him. That's quite a lot of news from just two little cards. And it's available to you over and over again, every time you bother to watch the cards at showdown.

Most home game players are as reliable as atomic clocks. They have their patterns of behavior, and they pretty much stick to them. Why? Because *A)* they're playing correctly according to their understanding of correct play and *B)* they don't think anyone is watching, so they feel no need to mix up their play. Big Bob pushes his draws, but his friend Large Rob only bets with a made hand. You know this. You've watched them both reveal their cards in more home games than you can count, and you've correlated their holdings with the way they bet. Now when Bob bets on the river, you can call or maybe even raise. If it's Rob, you know enough to get away from your hand.

Information is power! Information is money too, money *saved* through not wasting bets and money *earned* by extracting extra value. Also, information is fun. If you choose to embrace it as such, *backpredicting* an opponent (looking at his hand at showdown and then quickly reviewing how he bet it) can be a satisfying exercise in deductive reasoning. *Oh ho!* you realize, *Tiffany bet out on her straight draw and then check-raised when she got there. She can play aggressively and she can trap. Isn't that a thing to know?*

Keep your analysis intellectual, though, and not emotional. Ghosting your foes and backpredicting their showdowns will reveal to you all sorts of mistakes they make, some so laughably large that you'll be tempted to start viewing these benighted individuals with disdain or contempt. Dispassion is called for here. If you let a sense of superiority infect you, you'll end up trimming your own efforts to play your best. You'll stop watching every showdown because you'll start thinking you don't need to. Then you'll miss something critical, like an abrupt change in an opponent's behavior (because, for example, the alcohol has just kicked in), and you won't play correctly against him the next time you two clash. Also, don't forget to keep your discoveries to yourself. No one needs to know how smart you are.

By watching how your opponents play the game, you can usefully divide them into two categories: those who *think* their game and those who *feel* it. The thinking ones will consistently show you quality starting hands and solid, aggressive betting with the best of it. Though they're more likely to raise than to call, they know how to mix up their play. They'll trap and check-raise and bluff. They'll keep you on your toes.

The feeling ones will limp in with preposterously cheesy hands (I know I said dispassion was called for but, hey, nobody's perfect), justifying their calls with hunches or just the self-indulgent urge to scratch a particular itch. They'll raise too little, call too much, and chase too far. As creatures of habit, they'll give you a fixed target to aim at. They are not aware that in hold'em, self-indulgence equals self-destruction.

Take the time to divide your foes into these categories. It won't be hard. All you have to do is watch them play for a while. After that, your strategy is simple. Evade the thinking ones, attack the feeling ones, and you're bound to come out on top in the end.

9

OMAHOLICS ANONYMOUS

♠

The first time I played Omaha at Binion's Horseshoe in Las Vegas, I bought in to a $4–8 game with $100, posted my blind, and picked up my cards. Starting with A-2-J-T, I was delighted by a flop of 3-5-7. I had hit the nut low. When you get the goods, bet the goods, right? Even back then I knew that. So I raised every chance I got and hoped my hand would hold up. With luck, I could even hit my straight and scoop this monster pot—and a monster it was, with four or five of us capping the betting on each round. As one gleeful bystander put it, "We've got ourselves a shootout!" The turn was a 9, so was the river, and the fireworks continued on every street. Bet! Raise! Reraise! *Pow! Bam! Ooof!* I happily chucked my money in the pot, already thinking how good I would feel when they pushed the low half of that big pot my way.

I know what you're thinking. *He probably overlooked the fact that other players might also have A-2. He probably ended up split-*

ting the low three ways, or even four, and actually losing money on the hand. Oh, if only . . .

By the time I made my last raise, I had bet the better part of my buy-in, but I wasn't worried, for I had the lock low. "Turn 'em over," said the dealer. "Let's see what we've got." Oh, the smug look on my face when I grandly exposed my cards. Oh, how the color drained from my face when the dealer started pushing the whole pot in a totally other direction. I double-checked the board: 3-5-7-9-9. I knew my Omaha: two from your hand, three from the board, five different cards eight or under for a qualified low. A-2-3-5-7. How could I not have a lock low?

Oh.

Here's how.

At Binion's Horseshoe at that time they didn't play Omaha high-low split. At Binion's Horseshoe at that time they played Omaha high only. I had put almost a hundred bucks into the pot with a lock low *in a game where there was no low!*

I had no one but myself to blame. Sure, I could try to blame my parents for raising such an idiot kid, but *they* didn't overlook or ignore the brass placard beside the dealer, which clearly identified the game: $4–8 OMAHA. *They* didn't make the tragic assumption that all Omaha was high-low split by nature. *They* didn't throw all their money in the pot. Nope, that was all me.

Why do I revive this nightmare now? To prove what a nimrod I'm capable of being, that everybody makes mistakes, and if you know that the author of your poker book has made his share, perhaps you'll be more generous with yourself about yours? Nah, that's not it. Confession, then? Getting something off my chest that's been bugging me for years and years? Nope, I let it go long ago. Self-flagellation? Hardly. I can find much bigger sins to beat myself up about. No, I raise the point just to warn you that Omaha is a very tricky game, even if, unlike me, you know which version you're playing. Let's take a closer look, starting with starting requirements, just as we did with hold'em, and starting with the phrase *gung ho*.

Many people think *gung ho* means enthusiastic, and these days it does, but the original Mandarin expression meant "work together." When I tell you, then, that you want gung ho Omaha hands, you'll understand me to mean well-coordinated holdings where all your cards work together with the harmony of a commune, for example the *gongyèhézuòshè*, or Chinese Industrial Cooperative Society, whence we get the phrase gung ho.

What's a well-coordinated hand? In high Omaha, something like this: A♥-A♣-K♣-Q♥. Recalling that Omaha requires you to use two cards from your hand, look at all the tasty combinations this hand offers. The aces work together as a pair. The A♣-K♣ and the A♥-Q♥ are both drawing to the best possible flushes. The A-K, K-Q, and A-Q all offer straight draws. If you hold this hand and see a flop like A♦-T♥-9♥, you've got top set already, plus you're drawing to both the nut straight and the nut flush. You almost couldn't lose with this hand. It would take an offsuit 8, 7, or 6 to give someone a straight or else a highly unlikely draw to four-of-a-kind.

The beauty of a coordinated Omaha hand is that if it helps you one way, it's likely to help you in other ways, too. The danger of uncoordinated Omaha hands is that they don't have that strength. Suppose you hold J-J-7-6. If the flop comes J-x-x, (where x = an irrelevant or unhelpful card) your 7-6 is worthless. If the flop comes 8-5-x, your jacks are almost irrelevant. But with a hand like J-T-9-8, a flop like 9-8-x gives you two pair, the possibility of improving to a full house, plus eight ways to hit your straight. All your cards are still working for you.

High-low hands are a little harder to analyze because you have to consider both your high and your low two-card combinations or, as I call them, *packets*. Count the packets in this hand, A♦-2♥-3♣-4♦, and see how many you come up with.

Let's see . . . A-2, A-3 and A-4 are all live low draws. You could also call 2-3 a low packet, since an ace on the flop plus two other low cards will give you the nuts. A♦-4♦ is a flush packet. A-2, 2-3 and 3-4 are all low straight connectors. That looks like about eight packets to me. That hand has promise. But what about this one? A♣-4♦-9♥-9♠. I see only three packets there, and only if I count optimistically. The nines are a pair, and I could hit trips or a full house with them. But with the A-4, I'm looking to catch 2-3-little for a perfect low (unlikely) or 2-3-5 for a straight (unlikelier still).

Know what's a really bad hand in Omaha? Four of a kind. Pretty as it might look, a hand like 5-5-5-5 is dead in the water. You can't hit a straight or a flush or a low, and any full house you hit (with a board like T-T-T-x-x) would leave you vulnerable to, and victimized by, anyone with the fourth ten or any pair in hand higher than fives. It's a funny thing about Omaha that you can be dealt a monster hand like four of a kind—and absolutely have to throw it away. *Oh, why couldn't I have that hand in draw poker?* Even three of a kind is such a slim draw as to be a nearly automatic fold, unless it's something like A-A-A-2, where if the deuce is suited to one of the aces, you have both nut flush and nut low packets. Here you'd be playing your hand in spite of, not because of, its big pair potential.

Likewise beware hands with a surfeit of suited cards. A holding like A♦-T♦-6♦-4♦ looks handsome enough, but every extra diamond in your hand hurts the chances of your making a flush, and this hand doesn't have much at all going for it beyond the flush draw. It's a fold.

Then there are hands with three companionable cards, but one lonely unconnected card, or *dangler*, off to the side. Here are some ugly dangly hands: 2-3-4-K; 8-8-7-2; 5-6-7-J. Three of the cards work together, but one is just wasted space. Play hands with danglers and you'll be at a huge disadvantage to anyone playing fully coordinated cards. *Hands with danglers are ones you must fold if you hope to enjoy any sort of prosperity in Omaha.*

Many players don't know this, and others don't care. In Omaha/8, for example, most players will play any A-2, and hope to hit the nut low, or play any high pair hoping to flop a set, no matter what the rest of their hand looks like. If you practice patience, and wait for hands with five or six packets, you can pulverize these starry-eyed Omaholics who insist on getting involved with one- or two-way draws.

Because most Omaha players play too loosely, you'll get paid off handsomely when you hit your hand—but you're probably going to have to show down the nuts to win. This brings us back to Murphy's Law of Omaha: The hand that *could* beat you *will* beat you. It doesn't always happen this way, especially in home games where people may routinely overvalue the strength of their hands. But you don't want to have it routinely happening to you. If you're going to be drawing, be drawing to the nuts. A suited king or queen may look attractive, but it's toast in the face of a suited ace, and if there are suited aces out there, you *know* they're not going to fold. Likewise, if you're holding 5-6-x-x and looking at a board of 2-3-7-8-9, it's true that you have a straight, but you don't have the nut straight. Anyone with J-T or even T-6 will punish you for playing what's affectionately known as the *idiot end* of the straight.

Thus we have this practical strategy for success in these games.

Rule Book

In Omaha and Omaha/8, avoid going to war with second-best holdings.

Even your nut hands are at risk in this crazy game. A-2 is a good holding in Omaha/8; it's drawing to the nuts. But A-2-3 is a much better holding because it's drawing to the nuts *and* it's protected against *counterfeit*, where a low card in your hand is duplicated by one on board. With A-2-x-x, if the flop comes 2-8-K, you're pretty much done with the hand. But with A-2-3, you can take that same flop and still be drawing to the nuts. And if A-2 is good and A-2-3 is better, then A-2-3-4 will give you maximum protection against a counterfeit low. Of course, the board could still come K-Q-T, killing your low altogether, but hey, that's Omaha.

You're starting to see, I suppose, the raw power of the ace in Omaha and Omaha/8. You need an ace for the nut flush high. You need an ace for the nut low. In fact, if you'd like a good, conservative rule of thumb for Omaha, you might tell yourself to play no hands that contain no aces. Beyond that, here's your quick and dirty guide to Omaha starting requirements.

- Play gung ho holdings
- Avoid danglers
- Count your packets—the more, the merrier
- Don't be second best
- Above all, assume that the hand that *could* beat you *will* beat you. This will save your money, and your sanity, in both Omaha and Omaha/8.

The big news about post-flop play in hold'em, you'll recall, was fit or fold. That's valid strategy for Omaha too, and especially Omaha/8, where you're frequently drawing to only half the pot. *Get out while the getting is good.* Leave the optimistic chasing to the *flopheads* who never met an Omaha hand they didn't like or a draw too slim to take. What you want out of your Omaha flops are big hands or big draws: hands that are either favorites to win the pot without help or have good odds of improving past the current leader.

Try this on for size: In Omaha high you hold A-A-T-T and the flop comes A-9-2 rainbow. You're practically bulletproof. You have the top set, plus draws to the top full house. There are no good straight draws or flush draws out there. Anyone who catches up to you that way will have to hit runner-runner to do so, and that's pretty unlikely. Hitting a runner-runner flush draw, for instance, is a 23–1 shot. You don't want to be the one taking those odds, but you sure don't mind firing bets against someone who is.

Omaha high again, and this time you hold A-Q-J-9. The flop comes K-T-7, giving you 16 outs—any of 12 remaining aces, queens, jacks, or nines, plus 4 eights. Best of all, any straight card you hit will give you the nut straight—no drawing to the idiot end for you. *Okay,* you think to yourself, *sixteen cards left in the deck help me, but there are forty-five cards left in the deck, and twenty-nine of them are useless . . . bricks. I'm almost twice as likely to miss as to hit. That means I'm an underdog, right?*

Not exactly. You're almost 2–1 against hitting on the turn—but you have another chance on the river. I swore I wouldn't go all math on you, but just this once let's look at the numbers. Your probability of *not* hitting your straight on the turn is 29/45 or .644. If you miss on the turn, your probability of missing again on the river is 28/44 or .636. Your total probability of missing and missing again, then, is .644 × .636 or .409. Roughly four times out of ten you'll miss completely. *Which means that roughly six times out of ten, you'll hit!* True, you have nothing but a straight draw on the flop, but with 16 outs and 2 cards to come, you're actually a favorite, at 59 percent, to make that straight. This is what we call a big draw. You don't have the best hand yet, but you have excellent prospects of getting there.

If these calculations vex you, remember the trick of counting your outs and multiplying them by the number of cards to come and then again by 2 percent. Beyond that, if you play Omaha for any length of time, you'll quickly learn the difference between a fat draw, one with many outs, and a slim draw, one with damn too few. Take the fat draws, decline the slim ones, and you'll do just fine.

Consider: You're holding A-2-T-T in Omaha/8 and the flop comes 7-8-9. You have 22 outs to your nut low and two tries to get there. That's a fat draw. Discounting the times that an ace or a deuce counterfeits your low, you'll complete your hand more than 75 percent of the time. But what if there's only one low card on the flop? Say the flop comes 7-9-J. Now you're double-drawing to the low. You need to hit perfect low cards on both the turn and the river—*and* you're contesting for only half the pot. You don't need to know the exact numbers to see that that's a losing proposition. So we come to this useful rule of thumb

Rule Book

Don't double-draw to a low, even a perfect low.

Many Omaha/8 players simply can't wrap their brains around this concept. They hold A-2 in hand and cling to the hope of making their low, which will only happen about 25 percent of the time. Since they'll only get half the pot, they need basically everyone at the table to stay in the pot in order for this draw to be profitable. And at that it's only barely profitable. They'd be so much better off folding. But Omaholics have sticky hands and find it oh so hard to let go. So let me state this in no uncertain terms: *You'll make most of your money in Omaha from optimists who ignore or defy the odds, and you'll save most of your money by not being one of those guys.*

One sad fact of Omaha life is that a good hand on the flop can turn into trash on the turn. When that happens, you must be prepared to filter your analysis through objective clarity and get away from your hand. Don't let regret breed denial in your mind and keep you clinging to vain hopes. Good hands get overrun by good draws every day of the week in Omaha, and it is only the weak in Omaha who stand in front of the stampede.

Penny Stock holds A♦-A♠-J♠-T♦, a fine hand in high Omaha, one of the best, with its high card value, and high straight and double nut-flush draws. The flop comes 9-8-7 rainbow. She's flopped a straight and she bets right out, getting called in three or four places. The turn is a 7—and a raising war breaks out! What hands might they have called with on the flop that they're so excited by now on the turn? Pairs of sevens, eights, or nines, or any 8-7 or 9-7. One thing's for sure: *Someone* has a full house now. One other thing's for sure: Penny is disappointed. She started with a monster hand, flopped the temporary nuts, and saw the whole thing go down in flames on the turn.

She's not without outs, though, right? There are still theoretically two aces left in the deck and if she hits one on the river, she can regain her rightful status as queen of this here pot. If she stopped to do the numbers, she'd realize that she's worse than 20–1 to make this draw. If she *doesn't* stop to do the numbers, if she lets resentment color her judgment, she'll throw in three or four big bets on the turn and then, 95 times out of 100, *not* see an ace on the river. Hey, she might even call again on the river, if she can trick herself into thinking that *everybody* is lying or bluffing or vastly overplaying their hands. Why would she manipulate her analysis to her manifest detriment? Because she feels owed somehow. She thinks she deserved a better fate, given her fabulous starting hand.

You see this sort of thinking all the time in home games, and even in clubs and cardrooms. There's a technical phrase for it: *horse crap*. And people who let these feelings of entitlement stand between themselves and perfect play? There's a technical name for them, too. *Losers*. Don't be one of them. *If you're beaten and you know it, throw your cards in the muck and quietly congratulate yourself for seeing things as they are*. Realism, even grim realism, may be an Omaha player's single greatest strength.

It's easy to outthink ourselves on the turn. We overlook the obvious interpretation of events—*my opponent made his hand*—and search for excuses to stay involved. We see phantom bluffs or let ourselves believe that our foes are putting "moves" on us. They're not putting on moves. They're probably not that tricky, and even if they were, they couldn't count on us being smart enough (yes, smart enough) to fall for their fancy play. Anyway, this is Omaha. Made hands are a dime a dozen, and so are hopeless romantics. *You don't have to be tricky to win. Just make the best hand and let foes with lesser holdings call you down*.

The problem is more complex in Omaha/8, where you don't know if a made hand on the turn is a made high or a made low.

Suppose the flop was 4-5-K, and an 8 on the turn triggers a betting frenzy. Who's doing the betting, players with A-2 or players with 6-7? Common sense suggests that the low got there, because people are more likely to play hands containing A-2 than to play hands containing 6-7. But you can't count on that! In Omaha/8, especially low-limit Omaha/8, some people will play almost anything. Then again, some players will telegraph their orientation (high or low) by what they've done before the flop and the turn. You'll encounter, for instance, certain Omaha/8 players who consider any A-2 a license to raise. Others will raise only on pure high holdings like K-K-Q-J, hoping to get calls from a lot of low hands, who can then be driven off the pot if the flop comes without low potential. Here's where your backpredicting skills come in handy, helping you know where you're at when a two-way turn card comes and "a new county is heard from."

But again, don't outthink yourself. Just because the low got there, you can't assume that the high is left unattended. If a lot of people have seen the flop, you have to figure that all relevant draws are covered. With a flop of 7♦-8♥-K♦, for example, a turn card like the 4♦ will make the low *and* the straight *and* the flush. If you've made the straight, you'd like to believe that everyone else is going low and no one has the flush. That's a sunny interpretation, but not a particularly savvy one. What's called for here is a healthy dose of pessimism. If there are three suited cards on board, believe that there's a flush. If the board pairs, figure there's a full house. If you're on the low end of the straight, fear the high end. Sure, you'll throw away winners from time to time, but you won't throw off dozens of bets in situations where you're already drawing dead.

It's not all bad news in Omaha, of course. Sometimes you'll find yourself in favorable situations on the turn. One of the most pleasant of these is when you have a made hand plus a draw to a better hand or, in the case of Omaha/8, the other side of the pot. Suppose you hold A♥-2♦-K♥-3♠. After the turn, the board is a very hospitable 4♥-6♥-8♦-9♠. You already have a lock low, and thanks to the 3, you can't even be counterfeited. The low half of the pot is yours, and you're free rolling for the high half as well. If a nonpair heart comes, you'll have the lock low *and* the lock high. If the last card is the 8♥ or 9♥, well, maybe you'll lose to a full house, but you'll still have the low half of the pot to call your own.

Or you could hold that same hand and be looking at a board like Q♥-J♠-T♦-3♣. No low is possible, but you have the nut straight *and* you're drawing to the nut flush. You own about three-quarters of the deck. Anything that doesn't pair the board will either leave you with the best straight or promote you to the best flush. This is a time to get in as many bets as possible. You're guaranteed to get action from anyone else holding the A-K, but they don't have the nut flush redraw that you have.

A word of warning: *Don't get upside down in this situation.* Don't get into a raising war when you have the temporary nuts but someone else with the same hand is also free rolling to a better hand. If you and your opponent have identical hands, you can't make any more money by betting, since you'll end up splitting the pot. But if he has the flush draw backing up his nut straight, he could get lucky and win the whole pot. Moral of the story: *Don't put any bets in where the best you can hope for is to get those same bets back. Be the one on the* free roll *or just don't raise.*

Likewise, you don't want to go crazy betting your nut lows on the turn or the river if there's a decent chance that someone else has the same nut low. Say you hold A-2-x-x and the board shows 3-5-9-8-K. You have the nut low, but someone else may also have it, since everyone likes their A-2 starts as much as you do. If that's the case, you'll end up winning only a quarter of the pot, and any bets you make with fewer than four people in the pot will actually end up costing you money. Be sensitive to overheated action from other players. If you feel they're betting the same nut hand as yours, just call them down.

Omaha is an easy game to understand if you bother to study it with vigor. And it's an easy game to get completely wrong if you're lazy in your approach. People love it. They *think* they get it. They thrill to the myriad combinations that their four-card starting hands afford. They *love* to flop the nuts. They call with second-best hands and chase with ridiculously slender odds. All of these factors, taken as a whole, make Omaha, and especially Omaha/8, a profitable game for the disciplined, knowledgeable player. Introduce it to your home poker pals. Turn them into Omaholics. Stay out of problem situations, put others in them, and you can definitely reap the rewards.

10

SEVENLY STUDLY

♠

The first poker book I ever read was George Percy's *7 Card Stud: The Waiting Game*. Right there in the title, George put forth his philosophy. Wait, be patient. Good cards are coming and bad cards are beneath contempt. Armed with this wisdom, I sallied forth into the quarter-ante games of downtown Las Vegas, where I discovered, shockingly, that just by sticking to my starting requirements, I could play almost forever on almost no money and, what's more, put myself in a position to win every time I elected to enter a pot. It's a point I've made over and over in this book, and now that I think about it, I must have learned it from Percy in the first place. In seven-stud—in almost any form of poker—*a good start is a critically valuable asset.*

So what constitutes a good start in seven-stud? Well, the best initial holding is three of a kind, or *rolled-up trips*, something like (7♣-7♠)-7♥. Any set of rolled-up trips is a powerhouse hand, and you should push it hard. It's worth mentioning at this point that some players shy away from driving their premium holdings. They want to lure other players into the pot and so extract maximum value from their most valuable hands. This slow playing has a certain tactical application—but that's not why people do it!

Big hands come along infrequently. How infrequently? About one quarter of one percent of all seven-stud hands we're dealt will be rolled-up trips. No wonder we want to win with these beauties. They're rare and wonderful and terribly, terribly strong. Trouble is, we might not just *want* to win, we might feel like we *deserve* to win. Haven't we been patient? Haven't we played the waiting game? Doesn't the universe owe us a big pot to go with this big hand? Nope. The universe doesn't owe us anything but an education, and it gives us lessons every day. Sad is the stud player who slow-played his trips just long enough for straight draws or flush draws to get on the hook, then get there and send those marvelous trips crashing down to defeat. What should he have done instead? Raise! Run the risk of folding the field and winning almost nothing. It's better to win a small pot than to lose a big one, especially when your strategic thinking is skewed by the creeping sense of entitlement that seems to accompany monster hands.

Let's not kid ourselves. Rolled-up trips is a huge hand. It's so far out ahead of most other hands that you can afford to slow down a little. Slow down, but don't stop. You won't build a big pot if you don't bet anyone into it, right? Or, to look at it another way, if you have a big hand and they don't, they're making a mistake to call when you bet. How will they make that mistake if you don't give them the chance?

Bottom line: *Go ahead and adjust your betting if you think you can suck people into the pot and still come out with the best hand*. Just don't do it for the sake of getting all warm and fuzzy about turning a monster hand into a monster pot. Maybe you will, maybe not, but in any case this should be your goal. *Maximize value, not joy.* We've already talked about the difference between *thinking* and *feeling* players. When you let entitlement seduce you into slow-playing a big hand because you *just can't stand* to squander it on a puny little fold-out, you've slipped over from thinking into feeling. You're serving the wrong goals.

Well, rolled-up trips come along so rarely that you really won't have to worry too much about how you play them or misplay them. You're about a hundred times more likely to find yourself with an *open pair* or *hidden pair*, plus kicker. An open pair is something like (5-A)-A, whereas a hidden pair would be (A-A)-5. You can see right away that the hidden pair has extra muscle because its strength is well concealed. If your foes see you betting with an ace as your door card, they can reasonably put you on a pair of aces, but if you come out swinging with that visible 5, they won't know where you're at. Do you have a pair? Three to a straight? Three to a flush? Deception is on your side.

Perception is on your side as well, *if* you choose to use it. In a full game of seven-stud, you have seven other players' first cards to consider beside your own, and the relative strength or weakness of your starting pair depends a great deal on what everyone else happens to hold. Suppose, for example, you hold (J-J)-K. With a high pair and a high kicker, you're feeling pretty frisky until you look around the table and see these door cards: K . . . J . . . 7 . . . J . . . K . . . 3 . . . A. Your jacks are dead. There are none left for you to catch. Your king is barely breathing, with only one left in the deck. The best hand you can hope to improve to is two pair, and then only if you catch the sole remaining, or *case*, king. This is why we say . . .

Rule Book

Seven-card stud is a game of *live cards*. If your cards aren't live, get out of the pot.

If your pair cards and your kicker are sufficiently live, the next thing you want to examine is their rank relative to the rest of the board. In the best of circumstances you have something like (K-A)-K, where both your pair and your kicker are higher than any other card you see. But if you have a middle pair and middle kicker, like (7-8)-8, and you're facing several door cards better than yours, this is a hand you should muck. Here's a secret many seven-card stud players never catch on to: *Just because you have a pair doesn't necessarily mean you have a good hand or even a playable one.* People who routinely play small pairs with small kickers routinely end up losing to bigger pairs and bigger kickers. It only makes sense when you think about it. If you play top pairs only, who can sneak in above you?

Must you really be afraid of dominating door cards? You sure should, especially once you realize that two-thirds of the time your opponent's pair will be the rank of his door card. True? Yes, true. There are three possible combinations for a pair and a kicker in a starting seven-stud hand, for example (A♦-A♣)-2♥, (A♦-2♥)-A♣, (2♥-A♣)-A♦, and, as you can see, in only one of these cases is the pair concealed. Therefore, two times out of three, in a sense, what you see is what you get.

(This same principle, by the way, reveals why we almost never seem to be in the fastest checkout line at the supermarket. If there are five checkout lines, we have four chances out of five not to be in the fastest line. No wonder we get testy, or maybe that's just me.)

Now you see the real value of having your own pairs, particularly your big pairs, concealed. If your foe figures you for a pair, he's naturally more likely to put you on a pair of your door card's rank. With a hidden pair and a big kicker, you have both the apparent strength of the big door card and the hidden strength of the concealed pair. If all your cards are completely live, you can easily improve to a big two pair or, better still, a well-concealed three of a kind. This, again, argues for paying attention to everyone else's board cards and making sure that your hand is live, live, live.

As the hand develops, it may come to pass that a card you didn't care about earlier has become important to you now, maybe not even for your own hand, but for someone else's. Suppose it's just you and Doc on seventh street (the final card in seven stud) and you think he's looking for a ten for a straight. Are his tens live? Or did some get folded way back on third street? In a perfect world you'd have a perfect memory. I certainly don't. To help myself retain the important information of folded door cards, I developed the *Yankee Doodle* method of gluing my focs' starts into my short-term memory.

When the hand is first dealt, I take a swift glance around the table and silently sing, *Yankee Doodle came to town*, only I don't sing those words. Instead, I substitute the cards I see, starting with the one on my left and going clockwise around the table. Now I have a little tune planted in my brain, a tune I can count on to stay put for at least the length of a poker hand. Later, when I'm trying to recall whether those tens are live or dead, I can just "replay the tape," silently singing, for example, *Four, six, queen, queen, jack, ten, trey,* or whatever the cards happen to be.

You don't have to use this method, but you certainly should use *some* method, because the play of hands in stud is greatly influenced by what cards have fallen and what cards remain in the deck. This is not an issue in hold'em or other community card games, where there are no exposed spent cards to worry about. Here in stud, that's knowledge you need, and knowledge you'll only have if you pay attention, and if you find a way to store and retrieve the information available to you.

If you start with a pair, you mostly just care about your pair cards and kicker cards, but when you start to contemplate your straight draws, the problem compounds. Suppose you hold (J-T)-9. A quick *Yankee Doodle* tour reveals that no one's showing an eight or a queen. Good news for you, since you'll need one or another of those cards to make your straight. But what about sevens and kings? You'll need one or another of those as well. Now you have twice as many ranks to keep track of. You have to think ahead and ask yourself, *If I hit my eight, will I still have live sevens to draw to?*

Or how about a flush? Suppose you start with three to a flush and see two cards of your suit out. Can you still continue? What if three are dead? How about four? Well, while I certainly wouldn't draw to my flush with four cards of my suit spoken for, I really can't give you too many hard-and-fast rules about "how live is live?" I don't know how many opponents you face; what their starting requirements are, if any; whether they can successfully bluff; whether *you* can successfully bluff; what are your chances of hitting a backdoor something (like two pair if you're drawing to a flush); whether *that* hand would be good; and so on. That's why cowardly poker experts like me love to say, "It depends." How you proceed through a seven-stud hand depends on the evidence you face at the time.

If you haven't improved by fifth street (your third up-card is seven stud), you're generally correct to fold. Why? Because you now have to hit perfect on both sixth street and seventh street to make your hand. Say you started with three to a flush. If you caught bricks on fourth street and fifth street, you need to catch runner-runner suited cards, and depending on how many cards in your suit are already out, that's at least a 23–1 shot. Many smart stud players, by the way, will dump their straight draws or flush draws on *fourth* street if they don't improve, and you wouldn't be wrong to follow that plan. In fixed-limit stud, the bet size doubles on sixth street, which means that you'll be facing double bets from here on out. In high-low split games where there's a bet af-ter the declare, climbing uphill after fifth street is just murder! You'll end up paying and paying and paying for a chance to win half the pot, with a hand that might already be dead or in critical condition.

Here's a chart of hands you should consider calling with in seven-card stud, and also where you'll need to be on fifth street in order to continue to play. Notice that three of a kind is the only hand that doesn't need immediate help in order to stick around. That's because no matter what cards come on fourth or fifth street, you're still just one card away from hitting a full house on sixth or seventh street. With all the other hands, if you're not within shouting distance of a made hand after fifth street, your cards are in the muck and you are busy ghosting your foes.

Third Street Holding *minimum required to enter the pot*	Fifth Street Holding *minimum required to continue*
Three of a kind	Three of a kind
Three to a straight flush	Four to a straight or four to a flush
Three to a high flush	Four to a flush
Hidden or open high pair (kings or aces)	Two pair or trips
Hidden medium-high pair (T through Q)	Two pair or trips
Three to a high straight	Open-ended straight draw
Three high cards (T through A)	Pair or open-ended straight draw

These are pretty strict guidelines. They don't allow you to play low straight or flush draws, or low pairs. You can loosen up some if your poker night foes will enter the pot with any three random cards, but don't loosen up too much. Remember that tightness is a continuum and you always want to be on the tight end of the scale relative to the field. If you follow this start chart religiously, you might end up throwing away some potential winners, but at least you'll avoid getting involved with third-rate hands like (6-5)-8 and fourth-rate hands like (T-7)-3, and you'll have a strategy for wriggling off the hook before things get messy on the later streets.

Why don't you see low pairs or low straight or flush starts in these charts? Because hands like that are doubly dangerous. They have no high card value, so they run the risk of being dominated by higher holdings of the same type. And when you do make your hand and find yourself going up against a bigger set or straight or flush, it'll cost you *lots* of money. Since you have to be afraid of higher holdings, you won't be able to bet aggressively, but you might have to call someone else's aggressive betting. Hands like this, then, will either be small winners or big losers. It's best just not to get involved.

Also, just because a hand is theoretically playable, you're never too far wrong to let any holding go. Consider the case of three un-related high cards. If I hold (A-K)-J and my jack is the highest card onboard, I'll occasionally take a flier on this hand, especially if I know my opponents to be loose enough to play low pairs or flat-out rags. I'm hoping to catch another big card suited to my jack and build a dangerous-looking board that will scare my opponents into folding. But I want to stress that this is *not* a good hand. It can be exploited situationally, but that's all. Just because you *can* play doesn't mean you *must*.

Okay, then, here are the main points to consider in starting and continuing with hands in seven-card stud.

- Bet your big hands aggressively.
- Make sure your cards are *live*. Even a big pair is worthless if the other cards of that rank have already fallen.
- Keep track of exposed cards, thinking not just about the ones you need, but the ones your foes seem to need as well.
- Hidden pairs are better than open pairs.
- It's okay to play high straight draws and high flush draws, but only continue to play if you improve on the fourth card or fifth at the latest.
- Stay tight and stay patient to stay a winner.

Seven-card stud. It's not called the waiting game for nothing.

11

HIGH-LOW STUD STRATEGIES

♠

Split-pot stud games are popular at most poker nights, and it's worth looking for some tactical approaches here, a task made rather more difficult by the fact that tactics appropriate to one high-low stud version might not be at all right for another. Nevertheless I'll try to give you some tricks you can use and lines of thought appropriate to the myriad split-pot games that dot the home game horizon.

♦ ♦ ♦ Low-Draw Bias

It's useful to note that in all versions of high-low split games, players are generally more likely to chase low than to chase high. They'll get more enthusiastic about low draws than high ones, push them harder, and stay with them longer. Their motivation for this is exactly: *A)* right and *B)* wrong. They're correct in playing for low, in that it's easier to make a (notionally) playable low than it is to make a playable high. Players holding something like (A-7)-8 consider themselves a virtual lock to complete their low. (They may be overlooking the possibility of facing a better low, and we hope they are because that's one of the ways we'll beat them.) On the other hand, many players chase lows just because they feel naturally unlucky and consider it their destiny to be dealt garbage. Chasing low hands gives them a (flawed) rationale for playing garbage, and for believing that their garbage will hold up.

Do players really feel naturally unlucky? Sure—because players *are* naturally unlucky. It's much easier to miss a draw than to make one, so everyone in poker encounters negative outcomes much more frequently than positive ones. A weak-minded player, prone to confirmation bias, will overlook this normal order of things and conclude that he gets good cards less frequently than the other guy. When he gets low cards in a split-pot game, those cards fit neatly into his failure orientation. Away he goes, chasing lows till the cows come (lowing) home. Even if he has (K-2)-3 to start, he still figures he can *Miss, miss, miss,* which, in his mind, equals *Hit, hit, hit.*

Once again we see a player looking for any excuse to get involved with the hand. Don't look for an excuse to get involved. Look for an excuse *not* to get involved. Take pride in your ability to resist inferior holdings. *Restrict your low starts not just to possible lows but to excellent lows.* In seven-card games, you're looking specifically for three cards ranked seven or lower, where at least two are wheel cards, ace through five, and, ideally, one is an ace.

Aces, being the best high and best low card, and the only card to swing both ways, hold a special place in the hearts of split-stud players. Eights, on the other hand, are considered by many top-flight players a must to avoid. With eights, they point out, you can't make hands better than high lows or low highs. These two observations taken together lead to the following useful rule of thumb:

> **Rule Book**
>
> In high-low stud games, avoid playing a hand *with* an eight or nine, or *without* an ace.

Always note the number of cards you'll see in a given split-stud game, for the more cards players get dealt, the lower the low hands trend, and this impacts your strategic decisions. If you're playing five-card stud high-low, no qualifier, any two low cards represent a reasonable start because the best low could very well turn out to be paint-high or even a pair. In twist games, where players can redraw to their lows, the quality of the low rises dramatically. *Smooth sevens* are rampant (*smooth* being something like 7-4-3-2-A, where *rough* would be 7-6-5-4-A or so) and wheels are not uncommon. The greater number of cards being dealt, then, the tighter you should make your low starting requirements.

♦ ♦ ♦ Steal Opportunities

High-low stud games offer marvelous steal opportunities, and what you have is often not so important as what you appear to have. This isn't so much bluffing as it is driving—you're trying to drive out all other contenders for your half of the pot. You can often win half the pot just by looking strong, either strong high or strong low, so long as you're the only player going that direction. This is easier to pull off in five-stud (no qualify) than in seven-stud because you can make accurate judgments about your foes' potential strength. If it's five-stud and you hold (K)-5-7-3-A and your single remaining opponent holds (?)-K-Q-3-4 (where the question mark represents an unknown card), you know that you're a lock for low, no matter what his hole card happens to be. But suppose it's seven-stud and you hold (2-3)-7-2-4-3-(J). Looking across the table, you see (?-?)-6-6-5-3-(?). Your low appears quite strong, but you know it's no better than jack high. Meanwhile, your opponent could have a wheel or a straight, pairs, trips, or even a full house. You lack certainty, and run the risk of taking your *faux* low up against a real one. Be more likely to try your isolation steals, then, in situations where the quality of your information is high, even if the quality of your cards is not.

You may feel like you're getting a mixed message from me here. On one hand, I seem to be saying that you should play tight. Well, I am; I always say that. On the other hand, I seem to be telling you to be on the lookout for steal opportunities. Yep, I'm saying that, too, and the fact is, I feel very strongly both ways. If you do nothing else but play tight, you can absolutely be a long-term winner in home poker. If you play tight and tricky, you can be an even bigger winner, but tricky only works if it's backed up by awareness and perception. Some nights you'll find that you can get your foes leaning the wrong way all night long. On those nights you can mix drive-bluffs and isolation steals into your game. Other nights, when you're not feeling so sharp, just sit back and let the cards do their thing.

♦ ♦ ♦ Press. Don't Chase.

Beware of getting too frisky with high-only holdings in split-pot games. A hand like (K-K)-Q is a solid start in seven-stud high only, but climbs uphill in seven high-low against (A-2)-4 or (6♥-3♥)-7♥ or other holdings with two-way potential. While it's true that a high hand can scoop the pot if the low doesn't get there, it's also true that a low hand can turn into a high but not vice versa. So save your high-hand isolation steals for those times when the lows you're going against aren't showing aces or other backdoor high potential.

Low-hand isolation steals are less useful in games with qualified lows because you'll have to show down a real low to win your half of the pot in any case. Without this weapon in your arsenal, you want to play your low starts even more conservatively in eight must games. Look for those aces and stay away from hands containing even one unqualified card to start. Suppose you're playing qualified five-card stud *HLCD* (our shorthand for *high-low chip declare*) with a single twist and you start with (9)-2. To make your low, you'll have to catch three consecutive low cards, then twist away your nine for another low card, and catch that one, too. When you find yourself thinking that hands like this have merit, it's time to go home to bed.

Qualified-low games, on the other hand, give you a marvelous opportunity to be a bully with your high holdings. Suppose you look around the board and see a bunch of low door cards, while meanwhile you hold unpaired high cards. If you're playing in a game where people will go for low with any ragged low cards, go ahead and raise. You wouldn't do this in games where you'd only get action from players with low straight or low flush starts (and thus backdoor high potential), but here you can play the hand aggressively. You have two ways to win, either by improving your high holding or by isolating yourself as the only player going high. Plus, there's no guarantee that the lows will get there. If someone chases and hits, he gets half the pot, but if he chases and misses, *you get it all.*

♦ ♦ ♦ Use Your Right to Choose

Note the connection between the game you elect to deal and the way you play that game. Once every round in a dealer's choice home game, you get to decide what game to deal. With a judicious choice, you can actually deal yourself a measurable edge every time you get the deck. All you need is to choose the right game and have an accompanying game plan to execute if things go your way. As a dealer calling a game like qualified five-stud with a single twist, for example, you know that anyone who wants a qualified low is going to have to catch five out of six perfect cards to get it. You also know that some of your foes will chase, no matter what. Your game plan calls for you to catch a scary high door card and drive the betting, putting your optimistic foes once again on a chase with negative expectation.

Most players in dealer's choice home games don't make full use of this advantage. They choose games they like to play or games they feel lucky at. If you choose games because you know them better than everyone else or because you have an executable strategy for them, you give yourself yet another no-cost, no-risk way of advancing your avaricious cause.

As we've discussed, it's crucial in stud games to remember which cards have fallen by the wayside as the hand progresses.

This is doubly important in split-stud games, where you may have draws to both high and low, and have many different possibilities to consider. Not only that, in high-only stud, your only real decision is whether or not to stay in the hand. In split-stud, you may face the choice of twisting or not twisting, and you may have to decide whether you can plausibly win by declaring high or low, or going pig. If your foe shows (?) 3-4-6-7, you'll feel much more comfortable going against him for high if you know that all the fives are spoken for and he can't possibly have the straight. Here we revisit the question of which game you should call when it's your turn to deal. If you feel like your concentration is good and your focus is sharp, go ahead and deal a complex split-stud game that requires a lot of quality thought. If not, deal a one-way winner game, where your decision is reduced to play or not play. For my part, I prefer complex games early in the evening when my poker brain is fresh, and more straightforward fit-or-fold propositions when the night gets old and my mind goes stale.

Some players are just *never* good at this kind of thinking—morning, noon, or night. They don't know or don't care what constitutes a quality start. They don't hear or remember whether the low is qualified or not. They cling to the hope that a fortuitous twist on the end will save their hand, never stopping to consider that not having to twist is both a tactical edge and a money saver. They don't watch the cards fall, so they don't know whether they're drawing live or dead. Drop them into a complex matrix like stud high-low split with qualifies, twists, and declares and they're simply lost at sea. The more decisions you can put these opponents to, the more chances you give them to err. Since your profit lies generally in the mistakes of other players, you probably want to encourage as much split-pot action as possible.

♦ ♦ ♦ Chip-Declare Tells

If your high-low split games are played chip-declare, you can sometimes pick off a useful tell on whether your opponents are going high or low simply by the way they pick up their declare chips and/or hold them in their hands. In games where one-is-for-low and two-is-for-high, some careless players won't even bother taking a second chip out of their tray if they intend to go low. Others hold two chips in their hand more loosely than one, and the appearance of that "big fist" will make it clear they're going high. Still others convey their intent by letting their eyes wander around the table to hands of interest to them: They look at the lows if they're going low, for instance, to gauge how their own low measures up. In some cases, you can even snap off an audible tell, with the *clack* of two chips in a foe's hand making it clear that he's going high. Be alert to these tells and you may have the chance to change the direction of your own declare at the last second and grab an uncontested half of a pot.

Is this cheating? Investigating others' decisions before making yours? No. It would be cheating if they *showed* their declares, and you somehow stalled—and changed—before showing your own. But grabbing tells is fair game if your foes are sloppy or unaware enough to give you news you can use. Now, you may never get news you can use by this method; it may never pay any direct dividends. But if you go hunting for declare-tells, you'll necessarily raise your awareness and focus your attention, and that's a dividend in and of itself.

You may not be the only one at the table aware of this opportunity, so be sure to guard against giving away this tell. Whether you're going high or low, always take a sufficient number of chips in hand to declare either way. Also give equal attention to all your opponents' holdings, just in case someone has his eyes on your eyes. (You may even be able to transmit a false tell by giving inordinate attention to other players' highs when you're going low or vice versa.) Make sure your chips don't rattle in your hand. These efforts at protection may be unnecessary, but they don't hurt and they do keep you locked into the moment, so what's not to like?

Finally, ghost your foes extensively and never miss their hands at showdown. Once you know which ones have real starting requirements and which ones don't, you'll have another heavy lever you can use to move their chips to your side of the table. Simply put, a player who will only play pure high or pure low holdings and/or hands with aces and without eights is a much more formidable foe than someone who routinely gets in there with (2-2)-8, (K-Q)-3, or (5-6)-T. Once you know your foes' high-low starting requirements, you'll know whom to avoid and whom to routinely assault. Around here we have a saying: "Don't leave money lying on the table." Shrewd split-pot play gives you ample opportunity to rake in more than your share.

12

HOME POKER VARIATIONS

♠

We were short-handed one night. Steinlager had suffered some sort of breakdown—automotive or mental, it was never entirely clear. Carling had had a heart attack, and while he was perfectly willing to check himself out of the hospital and make it to the game, his kids had flown in from out of town to be by his side and he figured that ditching them would be bad form. Foster was chained to his desk. We'd told him before not to let work interfere with poker, but you know how some people are. And Bud? Well, with Bud, who knew? He could be shacked up with a supermodel, or he could be in jail.

So there we were, just four of us, long on cards and short on action. That's when *six gun* was born. Six gun is a six-card draw game, played high-low split, chip-declare (HLCD). With only 52 cards in the deck, you can't play six gun more than six-handed, nor can any player discard more than three cards—nor should they want to. If you don't have three working cards in this game, you don't have a hand. Since there are only two rounds of betting, we doubled the stakes, and found that six gun, while not that complex a game, provided surprisingly good action when we were short-handed. I think it was the sixth card. It added tremendous amounts of flexibility to our draws and got us all—even stolid, odds-driven me—hooked on the possibilities.

I quickly realized that there was a lot of information to be gained by correlating raises with draws. Someone might, for example, draw three cards to a low, but they'd be highly unlikely to raise with a hand so speculative. A raise plus a three-card draw, then, almost certainly meant that my foe was starting with trips and going high. If I found myself heads up at the end against this player, I'd declare low, no matter what I held. A one-card draw, to take another example, was highly suspect. What hand could a player hold that would be improved by just one card? A made flush with a low draw? A made low with a straight draw? You certainly wouldn't draw just one to two pair, not when you could draw two and double your chances of filling up. Most likely, the one-card draw was a thin attempt to disguise the fact of a made hand.

These are the sort of deductive edges you can milk out of quirky games, edges that are not generally available in the most popular poker games, where common moves and countermoves are known to all. You'll find such strategy tips liberally scattered throughout this section, for arcane games are the bread and butter of most home poker sessions, and you'll definitely want to take home more than your share of the bread. These games require insight and awareness completely apart from standard poker strategy. The better you know these games—their vagaries, nuances, and special circumstances—the better you'll do against opponents who don't bother to make such a study.

Since poker variations number in the hundreds, this chapter must necessarily be a sampling at best, but it will give you some ideas for new games to introduce—and perhaps stimulate your own creativity in this area. Feel free to explore and exploit that creativity. Remember, just because a game hasn't ever been played (or even thought of) before doesn't mean you can't give it a try tonight. Even draw poker got its start somewhere.

♦ ♦ ♦ Anaconda

"Two to the left, one to the right, come out punching, have a good fight." This is the battle cry of *anaconda*, wherein each player is dealt seven cards and must then pass away three cards . . . "two to the left and one to the right." Filling out your own hand from the cards you've been passed, you then throw away the two cards you don't want and arrange the remaining five cards in the order in which you wish them to appear. From this point forward, the game is played *roll your own*, which means that all players turn over a single card in unison. There's a round of betting, then another card is turned, and this continues until each player has four cards faceup and one remaining card facedown. Then there's a final round of betting, followed by the declare (plus a bet-after-declare if you play that way).

Anaconda is a popular game with the action crowd because they get to see ten cards (the seven in their hand, plus the three they get passed) before deciding whether to play. As you might imagine, or certainly know if you've played this game, the value of the hands gets quite high—and not just because of the number of cards you see. If Weezer is drawing to a low hand, it's in his interest to pass coordinated high cards to his foes: a big pair to his left; big paint to his right. Should his opponents be equally obliging in passing him low cards, he'll have a quality low hand and a chance for maximum profit when, thanks to his help, they start raising against each other with quality highs.

You typically see higher highs and lower lows in anaconda than in, for example, stud or hold'em, especially if the game is maxed out at seven-handed. For this reason, it's vital to stay away from second- or third-best holdings. *If you don't have a six-low or a wheel, or a big full house, don't chase!* Unschooled anaconda players will call along with straights or flushes, but you'll be better off pitching in your hand.

Just don't pitch prematurely. Some anaconda players lose interest after the pass if they miss and immediately discard all seven cards, rather than setting their hand as if they intended to play. This is a mistake, for it sometimes happens that many people (who know that it takes a quality hand to win at anaconda) will fold during the first round of betting and you'll find your ragged high or low isolated against two or more players going the other way. That's the catbird seat, no doubt, and it's often worth a raise to thin the field and see if you can set up this isolation play. In other words, *if you plan to bluff, bluff early.* By the time you get to the second or third round of betting, players are pretty well married to their hands.

Likewise, *if you're going to fold, fold early,* on (but not before) the first betting round. Don't let yourself get sucked in on the hope that your opponent is bluffing. With card values as high as they are in anaconda, he's probably not. Plus, the players going the other way (low when you're going high or high when you're going low) will be pumping up the pot, making it that much more expensive for you to chase a vain hope toward half a pot. Get out early, while your investment is still small. Good hands come around often enough in anaconda that you can afford to wait for yours. Get others to chase you when you have the best hand, but don't chase them in return. This simple strategy (along with always remembering what you passed and what was passed to you) will let you dominate and crush this game.

♦ ♦ ♦ Chicago

I spent an autumn in Chicago once, teaching at Northwestern University, and it was then I learned that Chicago has more different types of really crappy weather than anywhere else in the world. God knows why they named this game *Chicago*, for there's nothing in it to suggest crappy weather or, for that matter, hog butchering, ward politics, hapless baseball teams, or any other Windy City hallmark. In fact, there's nothing much to the game beyond one of two simple tweaks to standard seven-card stud. In *high Chicago*, the high hand splits the pot with the high spade in the hole. In *low Chicago*, it's the low spade (typically the deuce, not the ace) that takes half the pot. I have even known players to go "thirds" on Chicago, where the high hand and the low hand share the pot with either the high or low concealed spade.

How do you win Chicago? *Start with a strong spade in the hole, and fold if you don't have one.* You'd think this would be obvious, but many players will stay in all the way to the end on the uncertain hope of catching a winning spade on the last card. They believe that their chances of catching the spade augment their chances of winning with the best hand. What they forget—what you should *never* forget—is that the high hand is almost always playing for only half the pot here. If you're not sitting on a strong hand or a strong spade (preferably both), you're not likely to get enough payback from the pot to make *either* draw worthwhile. If you do start with a quality spade, ideally the best spade, it's often smart not to reveal your strength too soon. Let other players' hands develop, and let them come to believe (or anyway hope) that their second-best or third-best spades are good. Get them on the hook.

Chicago works as a home poker game because it's a no-brainer. Without having to consider *any* strategic implications, players can examine their hole cards for the boss spade and, if they have it, call along for a while and then start raising like nuts. That's not a bad strategy—it's the right strategy—but only when partnered with the other half of the plan: *No spade equals no hand. Fold, fold, fold.*

Every now and then you'll see someone essay a "spade bluff," betting as if they had a strong spade in the hole and trying to get mediocre spades or nonspade hands to fold. The problem with this approach is that it only works in games filled with sensible, aware players, players smart enough and disciplined enough to fold in the face of big action. These players are not likely to be playing Chicago in the first place. If they like the game enough to chase phantom spades to the river, they'll like it enough to call you down with weak spades, rather than give you the satisfaction of seeing them yield to a little betting pressure from you.

So . . . *don't bluff.* If Chicago gets dealt frequently in your home game, you will occasionally pick up the magic spade. When you do, you'll get plenty of action from the Cally Wallies in your game. When you don't, you can fold.

♦ ♦ ♦ Options

Options is an HLCD game that starts out looking like seven-card stud but quickly becomes something altogether else. In options, everyone gets two hole cards to start. Then three faceup cards are placed in the middle of the table, along with the rest of the deck.

The first player to the dealer's left can select one of the upcards or else take the top card off the deck, with an associated fee for each card. The cheapest card, for example, may cost a dollar, while the next card costs two, the third costs three, and the *blind pluck*, unknown card off the top of the deck, costs four. A typical options board lays out like this:

$1 card $2 card $3 card $4 card

After the first player selects a card (assuming it's one of the upcards), the dealer fills in the hole on the option board and the next player selects. In like manner, everyone around the table selects an option card. Next there's a round of betting, and then another option round, this time starting with the person two places to the dealer's left. Note: If the last person picks an upcard, that card is not replaced until after the subsequent betting round. Also, if no one has taken any of the upcards during one full round of options, those cards are thrown out and replaced with new ones before the start of the next selections. After four rounds of betting and four rounds of buying (with the first option shifting one position to the left each time), a final card is dealt facedown, followed by bet, declare, and showdown.

There are a couple of useful strategies you can easily learn and employ for options. The first concerns your two starting cards. If they're not well-coordinated to each other, and to the first slate of option cards, *fold*. With so many cards being picked over by so many players, you can count on hand values getting extremely high. Chasing with second-rate hands has a huge negative expectation, so it's very important that you limit your action to quality starts. The only exception to this may be if you can pick up, and build upon, an early inexpensive ace, because aces are such powerful cards in this, as in any, high-low split game.

Pay attention to what the other players are doing. You'll have trouble making a quality low hand, for example, if two or three players in front of you are snarfing up all the good low cards before the option comes your way. On the other hand, if they're all going low, they'll be leaving you your pick of high cards and you can often turn a bunch of orphaned jacks and queens into a high full house. The board will be of special interest to you when you'll be first to pick after the next round of betting. If there's a helpful card out there, you know you're going to get it, and you can afford to press the betting. If there's nothing out there you like, you'll have ample warning, and thus ample opportunity to get away from your hand.

Recognize that you'll sometimes have to make defensive picks. If the person behind you is clearly going for a flush, it'll do you no good to complete your straight if you leave a key card in his suit just sitting there. You may have to make a preemptive strike against his flush card and hope that he doesn't pick one up on the fill-in or by drawing blind.

Options is an expensive game. In addition to five rounds of betting, there are all those cards to be bought and, paradoxically, you pay less for cards you know than for ones you don't. Be very leery of that expensive unknown card off the top of the deck, for you can end up spending a lot of money without ever elevating your hand above stiff status. In most cases in options if you're faced with the choice between paying top dollar for a random card and folding, folding is the better, well, option.

♦ ♦ ♦ Smokehouse

This game goes by other names, such as *twist and shout* and *get it out of here*, but we call it *smokehouse* because we happened to stumble upon it the chilly night our host forgot to open the fireplace flue and filled his house with smoke. Smokehouse is a five-card stud variation, played HLCD, eight must, with not one but two twists after the fifth cards come out. Typically, the cost of the second twist is twice the price of the first. In this game, as in most twist situations, if you throw away a down card, you get a new down card, and if you throw away an upcard, your replacement comes faceup. There's a round of betting after each round of twisting, bringing the total number of betting rounds in this game to six.

Thanks to the beguiling promise of the second twist, there's a real premium on playing for a high hand which can split the pot with a qualified low—or scoop the pot if the low doesn't get there. I'm not saying that you should never play for low, since, after all, a low hand containing an ace can connect with another ace and suddenly turn into a powerhouse high. If you do draw low, don't *chase* low. As soon as you hit a brick, just fold your hand and happily contemplate all the money you're saving by not calling bets, or making buys, at the latter stages of play. The best place to be in this game is sitting on a made hand, either high or low, after five cards, and earning extra profit on other players' twist money going into the pot.

It's easy to know where you stand in this game. If someone is showing four unpaired cards on board, you know that the best hand their hole card can give them is a pair, and that the best hand they can twist to is three of a kind (absent, of course, straight or flush draws). This will often put you in a situation where you may think to save money by not taking a twist, but go ahead and twist anyhow. It's often better to buy a card and try to improve a hand that probably doesn't need improving. Remember that you'll get half the cost of your twist money back if you win the split pot—and all of it if you scoop. Sad is the player who figures that his two pair is good enough to win, only to see a foe twist to a straight and get there.

Because so much of a player's hand is revealed—and yet more is revealed by which cards he chooses to twist—smokehouse is a difficult game in which to bluff successfully. Nor can you steal lows by isolating yourself against the high hands when it's not just a matter of declaring low but of qualifying as well. The basic strategy for this game, then, is to press good starting hands, especially good starting high hands like pairs or unpaired paint, or hands with aces, and fold the rest of your holdings. Particularly avoid hands with nines, for a nine is doubly useless: too low to be a high card and too high to be a low. If you see someone knowledgeable playing a hand with a nine as his door card, strongly suspect a nine in the hole.

Depending on how the game is dealt, smokehouse can offer a shameless advantage to the dealer. Should it be the convention (as it is in many home games) that players twist in turn starting with the player to the dealer's left, then it happens that the dealer gets to see *everyone else's twist* before deciding whether, or which way, to twist his own hand. (And by the way, if you decline to twist at the first opportunity, you can still twist the second time around.) This advantage is so huge that some home games neutralize it by having the high hand or the last bettor twist first. Each of these conventions requires its own strategic adjustment. If the high hand twists first, be more likely to call the last pretwist bet if the high hand is to your left, not your right. If last bettor twists first, simply never be the last bettor.

In most home games, they neither recognize nor care about such things as dealer advantage. If that's the case where you play, do two things: 1) Try to deal smokehouse as frequently as possible; 2) Don't play iffy hands in early position. If you're immediately to the dealer's left, you know you'll be twisting first, so stick to absolute premium highs or lows.

Is it unethical for you, as the dealer in a dealer's choice home game, to call a game with such a strong dealer advantage? I don't think so. The other players can deal the same game if they're so inclined, and if they do you won't squawk about your position, you'll just adjust accordingly. If they're not savvy enough to recognize a dealer advantage when they see one, well, like the saying goes, "There's two kinds of problems in this world: my problem and not my problem." It seems to me that their ignorance is not your problem.

But it may very well be your bliss.

♦ ♦ ♦ Simultwist

Simultwist is a fusion word, the forced union of *simultaneous* and *twist*. It's an HLCD game built on the platform of six-card stud, where every player gets a down card and an upcard to start, then three more upcards, then a final card in the hole. After all that comes . . . the simultwist! For a set purchase price, each player in turn may buy two—exactly and only two—new cards, replacing upcards with upcards and down cards with down cards. You have the option of buying no cards for no charge, but if you twist at all, you must twist two. The game can be played either with or without a qualified low, but it generally plays better without the eight must, because players are inspired to chase and buy (and thus build the pot), knowing that their hand can't be entirely killed by a bad draw. After the twist comes another round of betting, then the declare and showdown.

Usually the double twist looks like a good idea. If you have four cards to a low, or two pair or a straight or flush draw for high, the twist gives you two chances to hit your hand. Sometimes you have four to a low straight or flush and can draw to both a high hand and a low hand. The only conundrums come when you have a made, but mediocre, low and must choose whether to sit on it or try to improve or if you're caught between a low draw and a high draw and can't decide which way to go. A lot will depend on what everyone else has, or seems to have, so once again we see the advantage of being last, or late, to twist, and also the danger of getting involved with second-rate hands in early position.

I know I'm starting to sound like a broken record, but you'll serve yourself well in this game if you *stay away from sketchy starts*. In particular, you want to avoid split hands like 2-K or Q-3 and seek instead connected hands like 2-3 or K-Q or pairs. Your goal is to make a hand in six cards and not have to twist at all. Not only will this let you drive the betting late in the hand, you'll get extra value out of the pot every time someone else has to buy and you don't. If you start with a split hand, whether it develops high or low, you just *know* you're going to end up buying. Why deal yourself that disadvantage? Fold, watch, and use what you learn about the other players to defeat them on a subsequent hand when you're dealt a quality start.

Simultwist offers some good pig opportunities, because you often find yourself with hands like low straights or flushes. Also, as in Omaha, you don't have to use the same cards for high as for low. If your final holding is A♦-2♦-3♦-4♣-5-♦-K♦, you have both a wheel low and an ace-high flush—two pretty darn good hands.

Still, you'll want to proceed with some caution, since the two-card twist tends to promote two pair to full houses with dismaying regularity. You could easily go pig with your wheel and big flush, but if one of your foes is showing a pair onboard and a lot of enthusiasm for his hand, think *Half a loaf* and settle for your lock low. Remember, if you so much as tie either way, you lose all equity in the pot.

♦ ♦ ♦ Bughouse

Bughouse, an HLCD bastardization of Omaha, is a terrific action game full of beguiling possibilities and stunning reversals that keep people hanging on until the final card. To deal bughouse, give every player five cards and then lay out nine in the middle like this:

Players have two options in terms of the cards they may use. They must either: *A)* make their best five-card holding with exactly two cards from their hand and three from the board in any vertical, horizontal, or diagonal straight line or *B)* use *no* cards from the board and *all five* cards in hand. This is the sneaky part of bughouse, as it's not uncommon to be dealt a good low hand in five cards (solid highs are a lot more rare) which can steal the pot from someone who thinks he has a lock onboard.

After an initial round of betting, the dealer turns over three cards in either the top or bottom row, or left or right column, for example . . .

At this point if your hand contains a two-card combination of either T-8 or A-2 or both, you're sitting pretty with a straight for high and/or the nut low. But hang on, for this is bughouse, the home of stunning reversals, and things can change in a big fat hurry. After a round of betting, there's a second flop, which might present us with a board of . . .

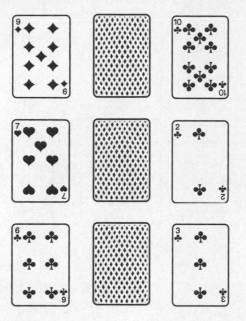

How do you like your hand now? Your straight has been superceded by a club flush as the (temporary) nut high, and your A-2 is now vulnerable to anyone holding an A-3 and hoping for a four, five, six, eight, or nine in the middle square. While you could hit a good low card, like a four or five, in the bottom row to regain your boss low status, you have to figure that your straight is now so much burnt toast, dominated by anyone in the multitudes holding a meager couple of clubs among their myriad two-card combinations.

Because the middle card in the bughouse layout can be used four different ways, the central row or column is always turned over last. After another round of betting, we see . . .

And suddenly everything has changed again. What's the best possible high hand now? Four nines? Nope. Four queens? Uh-uh. The best possible hand onboard is a ten-high straight flush in clubs; however, it's possible (although unlikely to the tune of 65,000–1) that someone is holding a higher straight flush or a royal flush in hand. More realistically, the possibilities abound for full houses, and anyone holding 9-3 or Q-9 or even 3-3 is probably pretty happy with his hand right now. The nut straight you started with is probably not even second best now.

On the low side, your prospects have likewise not improved. The queen on the bottom row has killed your redraw, and the nine in the middle ensures that someone holding an A-3 has a better low, 9-7-3-2-A across the middle row, than your 9-7-6-2-A down

the left side. Nevertheless, you swallow hard and declare for low.
What else can you do? You have no realistic chance of winning
high, and you didn't come all the way from Pacoima to . . . well,
you know.

At the showdown you find yourself facing only one competitor
for low. "Do you have the A-3?" you ask, half-hopeful, half-fearful.
"No," he replies, and your heart soars. But then he turns over his
cards: 8-7-6-4-2 in hand! You've been beaten by the bughouse
wrinkle . . . by the player's option to use all five cards in hand.

And what won on the high side? Queens full of nines. Well, at
least you were right about that.

Among fans of bughouse the question always rages: "What's a
good starting hand in this game?" We're all pretty much agreed
that ragged hands like K-J-9-6-3 are not terribly exciting starts,
but we've also all seen plenty of K-K-J or K-9-K flops that turn
bughouse losers into big winners. This is what makes bughouse
the Lorelei Stones of home poker. You're always just one perfect
flop away from a monster. So if everyone's going to stick around
with anything, how can the sensible player use his native intelli-
gence, charm, and good looks to carve out an edge?

First, *highly prize those lows-in-hand*. The nature of the bughouse board is such that, after the last cards are turned, you know
exactly what the best possible low can be. If you start with a
seven-low or an eight-low in hand, you'll either find yourself with
the nuts or know precisely where and how you might be beaten. A
low-in-hand buttressed by an A-2 or A-2-3 is even better because
if one of the flops comes, say, 4-5-7, it might defeat your low-in-
hand, but still leave you with at least a tie for best low using two-
in-hand.

Second, *look for highly coordinated hands*. High pairs supported by high straight or flush draws are useful cards to hold because a flop that helps your hand one way will likely set you up for help another way when subsequent cards are turned. Coordinated high cards are better than coordinated low cards for the obvious reason that they leave less room over your head for other hands to sneak in and dominate. If the first flop comes 6-5-7, that's a big help to your 9-8 holding, but if the next flop comes J-Q-K, you're dead to the jamoke holding A-T.

Third, *watch the board*. Bughouse usually tells you exactly where you stand, and it follows Murphy's Law of Omaha to an even greater degree: The hand that *could* be out there to beat you almost always *is* out there to beat you. Don't bluff, don't chase. The heaven-on-the-next-flop nature of the game guarantees that you'll get paid off plenty when you hit your big hands.

Should you play a lot of bughouse hands? Well, your opponents certainly will. If you can see a flop or two for a single bet each, then it's worth investigating the potential of your hand. But if you're experiencing early heat, it's probably coming from someone with a quality low-in-hand, in which case you should retreat to the high side of your holding, or get out altogether. *In bughouse, as in most poker night games, if you're just generally tighter than the field, you'll probably do all right.*

♦ ♦ ♦ **Bundles**

Bundles is vaguely like bughouse, in that you see an *awful* lot of cards, and you're restricted in terms of how many you can use. Every player is dealt four cards to start, and then *fifteen* (!) cards are placed on the board, thus:

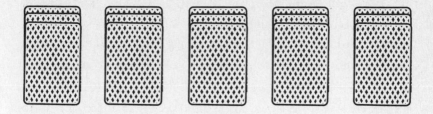

After each round of betting, a new three-card *bundle* is turned faceup. (In some games, the first three bundles are all turned up at once.) A winning hand, high or low, comprises two cards from a player's hand and any single three-card bundle. As with other HLCD games, you may use different holdings and different bundles if you're going pig.

You might think that with so many cards in play, high-quality hands predominate, but such is not really the case, at least not on the high side. You have to hit a bundle perfectly in order to make your high hands—three cards to a straight or a flush, or a pair and a kicker which both connect to two cards in your hand. Quality lows, on the other hand, are easier to come by, and *nut lows* are screaming to be exploited. If you start with any A-2, for example, you know you'll have the best of it so long as you don't see a bundle showing an ace or a deuce (to counterfeit your low) plus two other quality low cards. If you hold A-2-x-x and the first bundle comes 3-8-7, you're now only afraid of bundles like A-6-7 or 2-5-8. If one or another of those comes, watch out for aggressive betting and remember what's the better part of valor.

Strategy for bundles, then, is pretty straightforward: Stay away from speculative high hands that need a lot of help to improve, and push your A-2 (and especially your A-2-3) lows as hard as you can. As with all community card games, note what the best possible hand could be, and correlate the appearance of that hand with any sudden bumps in the action. If an otherwise quiet player suddenly gets all raisy upon seeing an A-A-K bundle, it's safe to assume he hit his hand. Don't dream; don't chase; don't pay him off "just to keep him honest." With six rounds of betting to wade through, you can't afford too much optimism. *Fold early, fold often, and wait for better days*.

♦ ♦ ♦ 7-27

This isn't really a poker game, and I'm loath to introduce it, but you see it so frequently in home games that I'd be remiss if I didn't at least give it a nod.

The first thing you have to do in 7-27 is forget the normal poker *what beats what*, because conventional poker values don't apply here. Instead, all that matters is the numerical value of each card. Deuces through tens are worth their face value. Picture cards are worth one-half. Aces count as either one or eleven. Players draw cards in an effort to get their hands closest to either 7 or 27, as if they were playing some mutant version of blackjack. If you start, for example, with two picture cards, you have a total of one point, and you're hoping to catch a six to make seven.

Each player in turn, starting from the dealer's left, is asked if he wants to take a card. Once everyone has accepted or declined a card, there's a round of betting, opened by the high hand onboard. If you decline a card on one round, you're still free to take one on later rounds; sometimes there's value in waiting to see what everyone else is up to before you make a move. The deal and the betting continue until a round comes where no one wants a card, after which there's one more round of betting, then the declare and showdown. In this case, your "low" or "high" declare means you're trying for either the 7 or the 27 end of the pot. Going pig is an option, but you won't do that unless you hold A-A-5, which is the perfect 7-27 because you can use your aces as ones for low and elevens for high. Just make sure no one else is sitting on exactly 7 or 27, or you'll tie and, according to pig rules, lose all equity in the pot.

It often happens that two or more players are equally close to the high or the low, but on either side of the number. House rules will determine what happens in this case. Some people play that the low side wins ties; 6½ defeats 7½, 26 bests 28, and so on. In other games, highs win ties, and in still other games tied hands split their half of the pot.

Ties can create an interesting situation, especially late in the hand when most players have dropped out. Suppose you're sitting on 27 exactly, with two other players in the pot, one who's clearly going low and the other who may or may not also have exactly 27. The low hand has a lock, and will obviously push in as many bets as possible, because he'll be making an additional 50 cents for every dollar he bets. You, on the other hand, are not sitting quite so pretty. If the other player going high has a losing hand, then you'll make that extra half a buck on every bet, too. But if his hand ties yours, then you'll both *lose* 25 cents for every additional dollar you throw in. The worst circumstance is where you know you have a better hand than your foe, raise at him constantly to make him pay to chase, and then end up losing money when he succeeds in making his hand. Sadness.

To avoid this sadness, simply don't play 7-27, or only play when you have a pat 7 to start. This happens frequently enough that any half-patient player can afford to wait for perfect starts and throw away everything else. If you're not *quite* that patient, try this: If you're under 7, draw aggressively in an effort to hit 7 exactly. If you miss, fold. Likewise, if you start out with a big number, like 17 through 20, and you're within striking distance of 27, go ahead and take a couple of quick shots at it. If you go way over, go away. If you pick up a lot of half-point picture cards, get out. Success in 7-27 demands that you make it quickly to a made hand, and then bet up the pot, charging as high a price as possible to those who choose to chase on. You never want to be on the other side of that equation, desperately trying to catch up to a made hand while the other players gleefully make you pay the maximum on every betting round. In fact, any time you find yourself competing for one side of the pot when someone else has a lock going the other way, you're probably better off folding. Why give anyone a chance to make free money at your expense?

The game of 7-27 is one where it really helps to know your foes, especially at the start of the hand. Who bluffs made lows? Who only bets when he's got the goods? Who slow plays natural 7s? Who will chase? Who can be driven off a second- or third-best low by aggressive betting? With a little courage and a little gamesmanship, you can put yourself in the position of being the only one to go high while the others go low or vice versa.

Hands containing aces are especially strong in this game because they afford you a second chance at your draws. Suppose you start out with an ace and deuce. You've got either 3 or 13, and you'd love to catch a 4 on the next card. If you catch a 9 instead, you now have 12 or 22. Your low is busted, but you're still drawing live to the high. If you miss *again*, getting an 8, say, you now have either 20 or 30. You obviously won't play your ace as an 11 now, but playing it as a 1 gives you yet another shot at hitting 27. Hands without aces lack this flexibility, and should be jettisoned quickly, especially hands like 2-8 or 9-paint. They're too high for low and too low for high. Don't chase, just fold. You need both discipline and cunning in 7-27, but discipline saves far more in the long run than cunning ever wins.

♦ ♦ ♦ Lucky Boy

This is a quickie little game unlike any other. Cards have their normal values, except that aces are high only and 7s, as we'll see, are quite special. Everyone is dealt one down card to start, with an eye toward making either a high or a low hand. The best possible high is A-A, followed by other pairs in descending order, and then unpaired high cards like A-K, A-J, and J-9. The best possible low is 2-3, followed by 2-4, 3-4, 2-5, and so on. After a betting round, players receive a second card, faceup. There's another round of betting, after which players may replace either their upcard or their down card for a set fee. Another round of betting follows, then the standard chip-declare.

But wait, there's more! Any player holding 7-7 (the so-called "lucky boy") automatically wins the entire pot. You can see the pickle this might put you in. Suppose you start with a 7 for a down card and a deuce for an upcard. Should you toss the deuce, hoping to hit a second 7 (more or less a 15–1 shot, depending on the number of other cards you've seen) or should you replace your down card, hoping to make (or anyway represent) the much more achievable solid low?

Most of the time it's not wise to draw to the second 7. You feel spectacular when you hit, but the pot almost never offers you sufficient odds to try. If you start out with something like 7-8, you might as well draw to the 7 because drawing to the 8 is almost as unlikely to result in a winning hand, and when it does, it will only win half the pot. If you're going to take a long shot, take it for the whole kit and caboodle.

It's easy to know what to fold in Lucky Boy, at least after your second card. Any hand containing two unpaired, non-seven, cards between five and jack has very dim prospects for either high or low. If you see no immediate steal opportunities—that is, if you can't get isolated as the only one going high or low—junk that hand, since any card you buy probably won't elevate you past second- or third-best. You won't feel confident driving the bets, which means you won't be able to bluff anyone out. You'll probably end up just calling along and losing to a hand you *knew* had you beaten all along.

In lucky boy, strategy—such as it is—is based on deception. Suppose you're dealt a pair of twos or threes. Your hand looks to be a low one, especially if you bet strongly and then don't draw. With any luck, all the other low contenders will fold, and you'll get action from players going high with unpaired aces or kings—who will then be shocked and dismayed when you scoop the pot by going high against them. Every now and then you'll run into equally concealed strength and lose to a higher pair, but, well, that's poker.

♠ ♠ ♠

Giant flying insects filled the house on the muggy June night that someone first dealt bughouse in our home game. It wasn't introduced to us by that name, but we quickly rechristened it, partly because it was clearly a game for madmen, but mostly in honor of the clouds of swarming critters that, fortunately, couldn't penetrate the clouds of cigar smoke we sent up like chaff in defense.

Now that I have formalized the game in print, it may have a more permanent or prominent place among the lesser arcana of home poker games. I'm happy to introduce it to you. If you go mad playing bughouse, well, "my work here is done."

But just because it's my game doesn't mean it has to be your game. Once you delve into the lesser arcana, you quickly come to realize that there's no end to inventiveness. You've been dealing bughouse with nine cards in the grid? Why stop there? Why not sixteen? Or maybe give players the option of playing one card from their hand and exactly the four corner cards (a variation we call *Georgehouse* because it was George's daft idea). Or subtract the corner cards and play *iron cross*, where you must use either the vertical or horizontal line to make your hand. How about eight-card stud? Has anyone ever thought of triple-draw lowball? (They have.) Multiflop Omaha? (Sure.) Simultwist smokehouse? (I haven't heard of it, but why the hell not?)

Poker variations are like languages or dialects. They evolve differently in different places and ultimately diverge so far as to become almost unrecognizable to one another. There's no one "right" way to play any of these games, although the rules and procedures I've presented here are at least standard practice in many games I know of. But at the end of the day, the way to play any poker game is the way that you and your cohorts find most stimulating and most fun. So introduce to others the games that I've introduced to you, but by all means don't let it go at that. Cook up perverse variations of your own or cut something new from whole cloth. The next great poker game is just waiting for you to think it up and deal.

13

THE NO-LIMIT REVOLUTION

♠

The other day I got a phone call from a friend. "You play poker, right?" he asked, which was kind of a dumb question, since everyone who knows me knows I play poker.

"Right," I said. "What's up?"

"I want to play," he said.

"No problem," I replied. "I can hook you up with a home game. How does $1-2 limit dealer's choice sound?"

"No. Hell, no. I want to play no-limit hold'em."

I was floored by this, by the audacity of it, because when I was coming up, no-limit hold'em was the *last* game a poker player tackled, after he had been very well grounded in limit poker play. I shouldn't have been surprised, though, because while it's true that no-limit hold'em is the variation of choice for the game's top players, it's quickly—and I mean at light speed—becoming the game of choice for poker's rawest recruits, too. Television is why, of course. People by the millions are getting their first serious look at poker on TV, and the game they're watching, the game that's inspiring them to play, is none other than no-limit Texas hold'em.

Now, conventional wisdom says that a new player should get crushed in this game. With the possibility of losing your entire stack to a single mistake, it would seem that a newbie or a rookie, the type of player most likely to make big mistakes, would quickly fall victim to experienced players who know how to detect, or provoke, and exploit such mistakes. Conventional wisdom says that no-limit hold'em is exactly the wrong poker variant for new players because it quickly strips them of their bankroll and drives them from the game.

But conventional wisdom has been turned upside down by television. So many new no-limit hold'em players are streaming into the game that they're literally overwhelming the game and changing its nature. Tournament pros have noted this and commented on it. They used to welcome inexperienced players into no-limit tournaments and considered their entry fees to be dead money. But when a significant portion of the field is new to the game, even the most savvy tournament pro loses the advantage of his experience. The sheer weight of numbers has morphed no-limit tournaments from chummy club events into free-for-alls. Many is the well-seasoned pro who has lately discovered the sad truth that, "You can't figure out their strategy if they don't have one."

Cash no-limit hold'em games are likewise undergoing a sea change. Now it's no longer a case of six or seven leatherbutts sitting around waiting to savage one unsuspecting innocent. Instead, with no-limit fever breaking out all over, equally (in)experienced players are sitting down together at poker nights everywhere and basically learning the game together as they go along. What does this do?

It levels the playing field.

And makes no-limit hold'em a playable game, even for absolute beginners.

When everyone is equally skilled and experienced, no one's at that big of a disadvantage, so new players need not go broke so quickly. No matter who wins or who loses, furthermore, the money stays in the hands of relatively equally matched players, so that someone suffering an initial setback can still stage a come-back. This would not necessarily be the case if a seasoned pro had taken the no-limit newbie's buy-in or bankroll and placed it safely out of reach by dint of superior knowledge and play.

Another factor is the advent of low buy-in no-limit hold'em. The Texas road gamblers who popularized the game used to play as high as they could, and newcomers needed major funding just to get involved. But new players with a TV-triggered taste for no-limit hold'em are sensibly looking for, or hosting, games where they can get their feet wet for the smallest possible sums. Ten-, twenty-, and fifty-dollar buy-in games are common. Some games even go for no money at all: Following the example of the free-play sections of internet poker sites, certain eager beavers are getting to-gether to play $0 buy-in no-limit hold'em, just to work on their game. They find—and this is key—that the challenge of mastering no-limit hold'em and the adrenalating thrill of pushing in a big stack provide sufficient buzz, even when there's not a cent at stake.

And when real money does come into play, even the smallest buy-in seems significant. We've talked about the gulp limit, the amount of money you need to put in play to feel like you're play-ing for a meaningful amount. Well, it turns out that no-limit hold'em has a tendency to lower that gulp threshold. A $10 buy-in may not inspire much gulping in a fixed-limit game, but put that same sawbuck into a no-limit contest, where you run the risk of losing it all on a single bad call, and the stakes seem magnified.

Providing further torque to the "bang for your buck" paradigm, we suddenly see an explosion in the popularity of home game *tournaments*, modeled, again, after the compelling poker porn we've all been watching on TV. Where such home-grown tournaments were virtually unheard-of a year ago, they've now become commonplace, with dozens of newly minted no-limit warriors gathering weekly or monthly, tossing maybe twenty bucks each into a tournament prize pool and playing for big glory, if not huge bucks. They like it. Check that; they *love* it. With the downside absolutely fixed at twenty dollars and the upside going as high as several hundred, tournaments provide a relatively risk-free way of getting the feel for the game.

Home poker players by the droves, then, are making no-limit hold'em, and maybe even tournament no-limit hold'em, the only game they care to learn or play or know.

With that in mind, let's take a look at the strategy adjustments you need to make when you first venture into the thrilling and demanding world of no-limit Texas hold'em.

♦ ♦ ♦ Two Basic Approaches

Most new hold'em players play too loose. They call too much and chase too much and see too many flops. No-limit hold'em punishes this tendency so severely that even the rookiest of rookies quickly learn to snug up their starting requirements. It's a phenomenon that veterans of limit hold'em find quite amazing: The threat of losing their whole stack at any time is effectively trending new players to an appropriate degree of tightness. In a limit game, they might decide to take a flier on a hand like K-3 suited, figuring, *What the hell, it's only one bet.* In no-limit, where anyone can bet anything at any time, the Damoclean sword of a major raise scares them off that hand.

Of course, not everyone knows what *tight* is, and not everyone knows how to evaluate the strength of their hands correctly. They may think that K-3 suited is a perfectly playable hand. But the first time they flop a king to that hand and lose their whole stack to someone holding A-K, they learn to treat that K-3 suited as the losing proposition it is. Likewise, the first time their A-7 gets dominated and crushed by an A-Q or A-J, they develop a healthy aversion to playing bad aces. In short, they tighten up, much more quickly and much more fully than they would in a limit game.

Meanwhile, a different sort of newcomer to no-limit hold'em watches all this snug play and quickly discovers the provocative truth that a big bet is a big stick. He finds that he can routinely bully timid players off their hands just by crashing into the pot with a lot of chips. He has a *willingness to bet*, a willingness that many new no-limit players simply won't have, for fear of putting their whole stack at risk. These other players may think he's bluffing, or even *know* he's bluffing, but they don't have hands that can call, or the strength of will to call (or raise) without cards. This ability to *overbet* the pot is one of the critical differences between limit and no-limit hold'em. In limit hold'em, you often can't make anyone respect your raise—after all, it's just one more bet—but in no-limit hold'em, it's possible to bet people off the pot.

No-limit hold'em players, then, quickly sort themselves into two types: those who wait for premium cards and protect their stack by staying out of trouble; and those, not content to wait, who prey on the Timid Timmies. Which sort of player should you be? It depends on the type of person you are. Do you like risk? Are you comfortable with gambling your whole stack at once? Or do you prefer to keep your variance low? No-limit bullies definitely run greater risks, but they also put themselves in position to reap greater rewards. Let's paint a picture.

Nick Rauchen is a tight, thoughtful no-limit newbie up against Vietato Fumare, also a newbie, but a reckless one. They have equal experience and equal $30 stacks in a game where the blinds are $1 and $2. The only real difference between them is Vietato's greater willingness to bet. Nick is in the small blind with T-T. Vietato is in the big blind with anything or nothing at all. Everyone folds around to Nick, who throws in $1 to complete the blind, hoping for a cheap and favorable flop. Vietato's having none of that, though. He raises $5, and now it's back to Nick, to call, fold or raise. Nick knows that Vietato is a lying sack of cheese, so he goes ahead and calls. The flop come A-K-3, and Vietato goes all in. Now what does Nick do? He still knows that Vietato is a lying sack of cheese, but even a lying sack of cheese could have an ace or a king in this situation. Tight, thoughtful player that he is, Nick decides not to jeopardize his stack against so unpredictable a foe as Vietato. He folds, giving Vietato a tidy little profit on his random hand in the big blind.

Yes, it's true that Nick could have flopped a set of tens and trapped the bluff-prone Vietato for all of his chips, and maybe that's the kind of opportunity Nick was looking for. But the odds against flopping a set are 7.5-1; Nick is much more likely to encounter the very sort of flop he saw here, a flop so scary that he can't call a big bet even if he thinks he might have the best hand.

The seeds of Nick's defeat were sown when he just completed his small blind. At that moment his hand was almost certainly the best one. Only pocket aces, kings, queens, or jacks would be better, and Vietato was better than 50-1 against having one of those hands at this time. A raise from Nick here would have very likely caused Vietato to fold, or at least yield the initiative, leaving Nick more in control of the hand on later streets.

Why didn't Nick raise? Probably he was afraid: afraid to run into one of those few premium hands that dominated his own, or afraid to face a big reraise from a frisky wild man like Vietato. He thought he was protecting his stack, but in fact, as we have seen, he was just opening the door to an untenable situation. Folks, if you're afraid to risk your stack, whether it's worth $10 or $10,000, you have no business playing no-limit hold'em. Those who don't feel this fear will simply eat you alive.

So we see that there are two sorts of players in no-limit hold'em: those who attack and those who defend. Your first job is to commit yourself to being the attacking type, for that's where real profit lies. Your next job is to figure out which category each of your opponents falls into, for you'll play very differently against each of the two types.

Defendy players are looking for cheap flops and low-risk, high-reward situations. They want to wait for a sure thing before making big bets, and when they make those big bets, you can be reliably certain that they have real strength—assuming, again, that they know what real strength is. Against these players you have broad freedom of action. Almost any time they don't raise, they're practically begging you to bet them off the pot. Many is the time in low buy-in no-limit hold'em that four or five players will limp in, only to face a big raise from an aggressive player in late position and *all fold*. Once more we see the advantage of proactive poker. When your late-position raise can pick up a pot the size of five or six big blinds, that's a significant stack builder. It also reinforces your table image as a force to be feared.

Not all your foes will be so accommodating, of course. When you find yourself up against attacky players, you need to adjust your approach. Don't bother battling them with marginal hands, and don't get involved in so-called pissing contests, where the two of you are betting and raising with nothing and whoever gets lucky gets the pot. There are better ways to deal with aggressive no-limit players. Dial back your own starting requirements. Fold where you would have called and call where you would have raised. And no, this doesn't turn you into a Timid Timmy. You're not like our friend Nick Rauchen who was afraid to bet his pocket tens. You have something very different in mind.

In this circumstance, you're not waiting to hit your hand, you're waiting to *strike!* You know that your attacky foe has the ability to get out ahead of his hand, and as soon as he does, you're going to pop him back with a big reraise and put him to a hard choice. This strategy absolutely requires two things. First, you must know who your tricky, aggressive enemies are, and second, you must be willing to make big bets if you think you can move them off their hands. You obviously wouldn't try this against an opponent who never folds, but many tricky players are alert to, and wary of, trap situations. Your big reraise says, *The trap is sprung.* It takes courage to spring such traps, but courage wins chips, so there you go.

Limit poker players quickly learn that a selective-aggressive strategy is a winning basic game plan. No-limit hold'em amplifies this principle. Be *more* selective, but *more* aggressive. Of course, if you find yourself a wolf among sheep, you can splash around in a lot of pots, knowing that the only one likely to make a big raise is, well, you. But people do get tired of being pushed around, and if you raise too promiscuously in no-limit hold'em, you'll find yourself regretting it when someone wakes up with a hand or simply decides to take a stand.

In other words, if you think you have the best of it, raise, and if you think everyone will fold, raise. Otherwise, basically, stay out of the hand. If you're flat-calling a lot of pots in no-limit hold'em, you're probably playing both too weak and too loose.

There are exceptions to this, of course. If you have something like J-T suited, or a low or middle pair, *and if* you're in late position, *and if* a lot of people have called, *and if* no one has raised, *and if* you can be reasonably sure that nobody behind you will raise, then you can go ahead and limp into the pot, hoping to catch a very favorable flop. That's a lot of *and ifs* though; you may be better off folding what you know to be an inferior hand, even if the size of the pot could argue for a call. After all, they can't capture your stack if you don't put it at risk by entering the pot.

Now that we're talking about stacks, let's examine the question of stack size. Unlike limit hold'em, where the relative amount of money doesn't come into play unless you're going all-in, in no-limit hold'em, and especially in tournament situations, the size of your stack, and the size of the stacks you face, is often as important as the cards you hold.

♦ ♦ ♦ If Your Stack Is Large

A large stack protects you in two significant ways. First, if you have more chips than anyone at the table, no one can bust you with a single bet. Second, your big stack is the aforementioned big stick, and anyone acting before you must necessarily fear that you'll use your tower of power to put them to a hard choice for all their chips. Consider your large stack, then, to be the potent weapon it is. Use it judiciously. Don't squander it on reckless adventures, but recognize its strength. It does give you certain freedoms.

A big stack lets you steal pots. When you raise with nothing, you're not raising with nothing. You're raising with the threat of raising again, and even if they feel they have you beat, they might not want to put their confidence to the test.

A big stack lets you punish draws. By adjusting the size of your bet, you can manipulate the pot odds that your foes face when deciding whether to call. Someone who is 3-1 against completing a flush, say, would be happy to call a $10 bet into a $50 pot. But if you can bet $100 at him, suddenly he's not getting good enough odds to call. If he does call, he'll be betting with the worst of it, poker's fundamental flub.

A big stack allows you to speculate. Suppose you're in middle position with a major stack and a minor hand like J-T suited. If you just call, players behind you with smaller stacks will be reluctant to raise, knowing that this would create the opportunity for you to reraise them all-in. They're thus more likely to just call (or fold) giving you a cheap look at the flop. Then, if you hit the flop (or even if you don't) you can use your big stack to muscle your opponents off their hands. Just remember that giving yourself a cheap flop gives your foes one too, which may put you in the unhappy situation of being trapped by an inferior hand you'd never have had to face if you had either raised or folded preflop.

A big stack, then, gives you both flexibility in your choices and a weapon that only you can use. Acquire one through judiciously aggressive play, and then use it as the powerful force it is.

♦ ♦ ♦ If Your Stack Is Average

When you have an average stack, the power of your chips is effectively neutralized. You have neither the hulking club of a large stack, nor the "when you got nothin', you got nothin' to lose" free-

dom of a small stack. At times like these, you want to revert to
your good, solid, patient poker and wait for the cards or the circumstances to present you with favorable opportunities.

Avoid going to war against large stacks because they have chip
strength that you don't have. If you're holding a fair amount of
chips, but not as much as your foe, you can put him to a reasonably hard choice, but he can put you all-in. In tournaments, this
can be catastrophic, because once you're out, you're out. Even in
low buy-in home cash games, where you can rebuy for a standard
amount if you go broke, you're digging yourself both a financial
and a psychological hole with every all-in loss you take and every
rebuy you have to make.

What you're looking for, then, is the harmonic convergence of
appropriate cards and appropriate foes. Ideally, you'd like to have
a chance to act after the big stacks have folded, giving you the opportunity to go to war against players even less chip-wealthy than
you. You may have to wait a while for this circumstance, but if you
have an average stack, you can afford to wait. The blinds will not
be so large in relation to your chip holdings that you're immediately imperiled. So tighten up your starting requirements and look
for the chance to make moves against smaller stacks.

Why must you tighten up your starting requirements? Because
both the large stacks and small stacks surrounding you will be
loosening theirs. As we've already seen, someone with a lot of
chips can afford to be more liberal in playing his speculative
hands. If you have something like 8-8 and raise into a big stack, he
may feel justified in calling with a couple of picture cards or a
mediocre ace in hopes either of catching a solid piece of the flop
or catching a scary flop he can use to bet you off your hand. In this
case your overly aggressive stance with an average stack is tanta-

mount to putting your head in the lion's mouth. Yum, says the lion; *ouch*, say you.

Small stacks imperil your play in the opposite way. Someone on the verge of going broke is looking for a place—any old place—to get his money in the pot, and he might not have time to be too picky. When you raise with your middle pair into such a player, he may feel constrained to call with something as weak as Q-T, but Q-T in this circumstance is not much worse than 50-50 to win the pot, so he's not completely out of line or out to lunch. One thing he knows for sure is that he doesn't have to worry about you betting him off his hand after the flop. His money's already in the middle. He is literally bluff-proof.

So with a stack that stands between larger stacks and smaller stacks, it's incumbent upon you to pick your spots with care. Remember that you can afford to be patient, but when you see an opportunity, seize it! If you're behind a big stack who has folded, for example, and in front of a small stack who's desperate, plan your attack and execute it. It helps to have a hand, but it helps even more to know your foe. How desperate is he? If you know he'll call with anything or nothing, then you can feel confident betting him all-in with your own semi-strong hands. Either he'll fold or else call you with a bad hand.

Interestingly, if he's not completely desperate, if he still has a shred of patience, you can afford to be even more aggressive in deciding to make your move. A player getting down to the felt is always weighing his prospects in this hand against the possibility of picking up a genuinely superior hand on the next deal or the deal after that. When you know your foes, you know how likely they are to go with "the devil they know" or, conversely, wait to see what's behind door number three.

♦ ♦ ♦ When Your Stack Is Small

Short stacks come with their own problems and opportunities. The obvious problem is that you don't have enough chips to bet anyone off their hand. A more subtle problem is your image. If you're sitting on a short stack, you look weak and feeble. Other players will figure that you're running unlucky or playing badly or in some other sense morally inferior, and they will come after you.

Moreover, you don't have much flexibility. With a large stack, or even an average one, you can raise preflop, or call a preflop raise, and still have a move or two to make on later streets. Since a small stack is likely to be all-in before the flop, it becomes, metaphorically speaking, the final bullet in your gun. You're going to have to pick your target, fire away, and hope your hand holds up.

On top of everything else, you're running out of time! You know that you'll have to make a move soon or risk being blinded into oblivion. In a tournament (one without rebuys) that oblivion is permanent. Once your chips are gone, hey, so are you. In low buy-in no-limit cash games, you'll have the option of buying more chips once you go broke, but that will only build you back to an average stack size or worse, plus it's forced you to rebuy, with all the financial and emotional fallout that implies. You'd really like to rebuild your stack without having to go back into your wallet, but the clock is ticking and you may not be getting much help from your cards.

On the other hand, your short stack means that if you enter the pot at all, you're probably committed to playing all of your chips. This is not the worst place to be in poker, especially against strong, frisky opponents who like to mess with you after the flop. In this circumstance, there will be no messing with you: Your chips will go in the middle, and your hand will either stand up or it won't.

When your stack is short, you have to strike a balance between committing your chips prematurely (going all-in with an inferior hand) or waiting so long that by the time you finally do bet your small stack, even winning the pot won't materially help your cause.

So then what sort of hands should you go with? Ideally, you'll pick up a big pocket pair in your hour of need, but since that's a long shot, you'll have to be prepared to make an informed selection from among a range of second-rate holdings. The hand you want is one that can beat one or two opponents with little or no help from the board. Hands containing an ace or two unpaired picture cards are reasonable candidates, as are pairs of any size. Small unpaired cards, even suited or connected, should be avoided, as you'll probably have to make two pair or a straight or a flush to win, and that's asking for just too much help from the board.

But selecting which hand to go all-in with is a last resort move anyhow. You have two better alternatives, at least in cash games. One is to leave the game while you still have a little money and a little discipline left. The other is to rebuy before you go all-in. In most low buy-in no-limit games, short-stacked players can rebuy any time they like—and yet they tend not to. When they start to get close to the felt, their thinking switches from playing aggressively to getting lucky. They don't want to take that next buy-in, so they hope that they can make an all-in stand that works. This is wrong-headed in several ways.

First, it leaves you short-stacked, which is the most vulnerable state a no-limit player can be in. Second, it sends the message that you're scared: scared to lose your money and scared to put more money into play, lest you lose that, too. Third, it costs you the opportunity to make real money. Suppose you decide to cling to your short stack, only to pick up pocket aces when you have almost nothing to bet and therefore almost nothing to win. Wouldn't you rather have reloaded before you hit that big hand? Remember what I said earlier about fear: If your fear of losing money keeps you from playing no-limit hold'em correctly, you probably shouldn't play it at all.

♦ ♦ ♦ Bet Size

In limit poker, you have no choice about the size of your bets and raises: Before and after the flop, they're one unit; on the turn and river they're two. In no-limit poker you have maximum flexibility. Though you're never allowed to make a raise smaller than the bet you just called, you can nevertheless choose to bet anything from a modest amount to everything you've got. With this in mind, the size of your bet becomes a major strategic consideration. In all circumstances, you want to ask yourself, *What do I want this bet to achieve?* Do you want loose money to call? Do you want to close out the field and get heads up against one opponent? Do you want to drive out the draws? Do you want to find out where your foes are at? Do you want everyone to fold? Are you bluffing? Let's look at these in turn.

Getting loose money to call. Small bets and raises have a tendency to invite players into the pot. If you know that certain foes are too loose, you can tempt them into the pot with a modest raise, figuring to blow them off their hands with a big bet later. Likewise, with a small bet you might be able to milk a few more chips from someone holding a hand inferior to yours, whereas if you bet big, he'll get scared and fold.

Closing out the field. Suppose you have something like J-J and someone in front of you opens the pot for a raise. You suspect that he has something like A-Q, or, ideally, a pair smaller than yours. Your most profitable play is to take on this player one-on-one, so you make a substantial raise, sending a message to the rest of the field, *Stand back, boys, he's mine!* This raise, then, is intended to get all the bystanders to fold. As an added advantage, the original bettor might also fold, closing out the field completely and winning you the pot right there.

Driving out the draws. You'll remember from our discussion of pot odds and card odds that a call is either correct or incorrect depending on the return on investment that the pot is offering. If you have an opponent on a draw, you want to make sure that your raise is big enough to put him on the wrong side of his draw. That way if he calls, he's making a mistake, and if he folds, hey, you win. Should you make a small bet here, you're offering him a favorable investment, otherwise known as *pricing him into the pot*. The only time you'd want to do that is when he can't beat you even if he does improve—when he's drawing to a flush, for example, but you already have a full house.

Finding out where they're at. Sometimes you might want to make a modest raise, a probing raise, to find out whether your opponents have real hands or not. I call this *active sonar*: pinging the target to define it more closely. It's common, for example, not to know whether a certain flop has helped your opponent or not. If you're first to act and you just check, you're basically surrendering the pot, because he can bet whether he has a hand or not. But if you come out swinging, you put him to the choice of calling, folding, or raising, and whichever action he takes will clarify your picture of his hand. The key here is to make a bet big enough to be meaningful but small enough that you can still wriggle off the hook by folding if he comes back at you for a huge amount or all his chips.

Getting everyone to fold. If you think you have the best hand, don't be afraid to win the pot right there. Make a big bet and encourage everyone to surrender without a fight. In can be disastrous to get greedy and bet small, trying to build a big pot. Suppose you have A-9 and you're looking at a board like 9-8-6. Yes, you have the best hand now, but your holding is fragile. Straight draws are rampant, and any K, Q, J, or T can give someone a bigger pair. You want to bet this hand big enough to discourage people from trying to catch up. Remember, when you get the goods, bet the goods. It doesn't pay to get too cute.

You're bluffing. Depending on how your opponents read you, the size of your bet can suggest to them whether you have a real hand or not. If they know you to bet big with real cards, you'll have to bet big when you're bluffing too. On the other hand, if they know you to be tricky and capable of betting small with huge hands, then you might be able to bluff successfully with a small bet or raise that smells like a trap to them. Always consider the pot size, since there's no point in making a small bet into a big pot if you'll only succeed in pricing drawing hands into the pot. A big bluff is the most nerve-wracking play in no-limit hold'em—but it's a thing of beauty when it works.

There are other reasons for making raises, and you'll discover them as you learn and grow in the game. In all events have a reason when you raise. A raise can typically either build a pot or narrow the field, but it can't really do both. Also make sure that your reason for raising is based on strategy and not emotion. If someone has just bet you off a hand and you come back firing on the next hand, your *take that!* raise is likely to be read for what it is: a reckless adventure launched by a hothead. Cooler heads prevail in every form of poker; a player on tilt in no-limit Texas hold'em is just giving his money away.

It's common for new no-limit players to make the mistake of betting too small. Either they're stuck in the habits of limit poker, where the raise is only as big as the bet in front of it, or they're afraid to jeopardize too much of their stack at once. Don't fall into this trap. When you raise, *raise*. Here are three useful rules of thumb.

1. If you're raising pre-flop, make raises that are roughly two or three times the size of the big blind. That's a bet big enough to drive out weak hands but small enough so that you can get away from your hand if you face a significant reraise. Make your raises of a consistent size whether you have a great hand or a good hand or a stone cold bluff. That way, no one can deduce the strength of your hand from the size of your bet.

2. On the flop or the turn, make bets or raises that are about the size of the pot. This will always be a substantial sum relative to the size of the pot, and it will keep you from betting too little and letting inferior hands come after you. Of course, you'll have to consider your stack size and the sizes

of the stacks you face but, again, if you consistently make your bets in this range, no one will be able to pick off the sort of tells that wildly varying bet sizes are prone to revealing.

3. Don't be too anxious to go all-in. Just because you *can* bet everything doesn't mean you *must* bet everything. The beauty of no-limit hold'em is the opportunity for finesse it offers, and while pushing in your stack is adrenalating and fun, it takes away your options. Plus, if you constantly use your stack as a weapon of mass destruction, you're just asking for your opponents to wait till they've got a big hand and trap you for all your chips. Pick your spots with care.

♦ ♦ ♦ A Few Words on Tournaments

To say that no-limit hold'em tournaments are all the rage is to do a stunning disservice to the word "rage." From a couple or three tables crammed into someone's apartment to moderate buy-in online jousts to major tournaments attracting thousand-player fields, the no-limit revolution is here. Whether it's here to stay remains to be seen, but if you find yourself playing in a no-limit hold'em tournament, whether at home or away, you'll want to go in with a game plan. Here's a quick-and-dirty strategy for dealing with the common stages of a no-limit Texas hold'em tournament.

At the Start: Don't Jump the Gun. When a poker tournament starts, it's easy to feel nervous, edgy, excited. This is especially true in no-limit, where you could literally bust someone out (or get busted out) from the first hand forward. My advice for this part of the tournament is *go slow*. Your stack will be large enough, relative to the size of the blinds, that you can afford to practice patience. Right now it's more important to get to know your foes than it is to play a lot of hands. After all, you'll only advance in the tournament if you win lots of chips at the expense of this very set of players. Restrict your starts to premium hands—big pairs and big aces—and let everything else go. Then spend your time watching your opponents very carefully. They'll be giving you lots of information on their starting requirements and betting patterns, plus other useful tells. You'll need to pay close attention to pick this information off, and if you're frisking around in a lot of pots, you probably won't be making the most of this learning opportunity.

Early Stages: Rebuy or Freeze-Out? Poker tournaments come in two flavors, rebuy and freeze-out. In a rebuy tournament, if you go broke during the early stages (typically the first hour or two of play) you can buy your way back into the tournament. In freeze-out tournaments, you don't have this option; once your chips are gone, you're gone. Playing strategies are greatly affected by whether the tournament structure is rebuy or freeze-out. Generally speaking, players in a rebuy tournament will play much more wildly than in a freeze-out tournament, since they know they're protected from busting out, at least until the rebuy period ends. You'll see a lot of players making large bets with improbable hands, hoping to get lucky, but prepared to rebuy if they don't.

Of course, the same rebuy that protects them also protects you. You can afford to be a little more liberal with your starting requirements. Especially be on the lookout for cheap flops and big fields. If many players have limped into the pot, you can limp too, hoping to catch a well-disguised big hand that you can trap with and win a lot of chips. At the same time, don't be too reckless with your stack. You don't want to get a case of *rebuy fever*, where you go broke and rebuy so many times that the tournament ends up costing you five, six, seven times more than you had originally planned. Most tournament players have a set number of rebuys that they're willing to take; beyond that number (three or four is reasonable) they figure, hey, it's just not their day.

Freeze-out tournaments require that you guard your chips more closely, since you can't replace them. In a freeze-out situation, be selective in the hands you play but aggressive when you enter the pot. Raise more than you call and raise a standard, sizeable amount—three times the size of the big blind is usually good. You want to win your share of uncontested pots but also want to be holding some kind of hand in case they don't all get out of your way.

Middle Stages: The Long Run. After the rebuy period ends, play tightens up considerably, as people are aware that they can't replenish their precious chips. Also, limits are going up, which means that people will start to feel like their stacks are imperiled and in need of protection. For these reasons, in freeze-out and rebuy tournaments alike, the middle stage of the tournament is the time to muster your fortitude and attack! Since players are more likely to fold hands they'd have played earlier, you should be more likely to raise in late position with somewhat less than perfect cards (or even with downright lousy ones.) Ideally, you want to "take over the table," to be the one who's doing a lot of raising while others are doing a lot of folding. You don't want to get too far out ahead of your hands, of course, nor imperil your own stack, but no one wins poker tournaments without at least a certain amount of naked aggression at the right time.

Also—let's be frank—no one wins tournaments without catching a little luck along the way. There are times when luck will run against you, when you make exactly the right move at the right time against the right opponent and end up, tragically, with the wrong result. Don't worry about busting out. It happens to almost every player in the tournament! Of this you can be sure: If you're so afraid of busting out that you fail to bet strongly when the situation warrants, you will certainly not win. Like the man said, "Go big or go home!" The middle stage of a tournament is the time for you to go big, because many players around you will be playing more conservatively than they should.

Late Stages: In Sight of the Barn. When you start to close in on the final table or, if it's a big enough tournament, the final few tables, you face a certain crucial decision. Having come this far, will you now play it safe and limp into the money, or will you continue to play strongly in an effort to win the tournament? It's a fact of tournament life that most of the prize money is concentrated in the top three places, so that's where you should concentrate your energy and interest. Yet many people are satisfied to play for any "in the money" finish. They're content, in other words, to win their buy-in back and not a whole lot more. This seems to me a pernicious sort of false economy. Of the person who's satisfied to put six or seven (or many more!) hours into a tournament, only to get back more or less the same money he started with, I have to wonder why he bothered to play in the first place.

Many of your foes will freeze up when they get in sight of the barn. They'll start playing not to lose instead of playing to win. Note which of your opponents are in this mode and go after them—not recklessly, but judiciously. At this point in a no-limit tournament, blinds are quite high and antes are also in play. It simply costs too much to sit and wait for great cards. You have to get in there and mix it up. The final joust is yet to come, and you want to go into that battle as heavily armed as possible.

The Final Table: The Final Frontier. The final table of a tournament is a unique place for a couple of reasons. First, everyone who's there is in the money. They know that they've overcome long odds and a large field to guarantee themselves some sort of payday. This will make some players play with more confidence, and it will cause others to become quite careless and sloppy. If you've been doing your job—watching and studying your foes all along—you should have everyone well ghosted by now, aware of which of your opponents to attack and to which you should give a wide berth.

If you find yourself at the final table without a lot of chips, you'll have to decide whether to try and fight your way back into contention or sit back and let players eliminate each other, giving you a higher money finish. This decision is dictated by cards, relative stack sizes, the quality of your opponents, the size of the prize pool, and many other factors. It's a challenging situation to be in if you've never been there before, and to top it all off, for the first time in the tournament, you'll be playing short-handed, then *very* short-handed, and then (if all goes well) heads up. This is one reason you see the same top pros finishing first in tournaments over and over again. They've got sufficient experience to know how to "close the deal."

While I can't guide you through the specifics of final table play, I can give you three concrete pieces of advice that will help.

Practice Tournament Play. Every online poker site offers no-money no-limit hold'em tournaments where you can work on and refine all your tournament moves and especially your final table play. Single-table sit-and-go tournaments are, in essence, final tables from the start. They're a great place to practice your chops.

Read What the Experts Have to Say. Detailed no-limit hold'em tournament strategy is considerably outside the scope of this book, but fortunately, there are many excellent books out there that can walk you through the process step by exciting and agonizing step. You'll find several listed in my "recommended reading" section. Track down those books or some of the other worthy titles out there. No-limit hold'em strategy is something that can be taught and learned, so there's no need to go in ill-informed.

Be in It to Win It. It's a shattering experience to put long hours into a tournament only to finish *on the bubble* (one place out of the money). To avoid that agony, many players will play way too conservatively as the final table or tables approach. Don't be like that. The big money and the big glory rest at the top of the leader board. No one remembers who came in tenth. It's better to play correctly and finish out of the money than to wimp out and limp to a second-rate payday.

♦ ♦ ♦ **Top Ten Tips**

There's much more we could discuss on the subject of no-limit hold'em. Scratched the surface? We've barely scratched the surface of the surface. I'll close out this section with ten top tips for no-limit hold'em play. They won't tell you everything you need to know, but they'll get you pointed in the right direction.

1. **Take Your Time.** When bets and raises start flying all over the place, it's easy to get reckless—but with your whole stack at stake, you can't afford to be rash. Even if you're sure you know what the right move is, take a moment to think it through. Many a bankroll, or tournament, has been lost by a hasty move.

2. **Snug Up Your Starting Requirements.** Hands like A-J or A-Q are often quite playable in limit poker because the price of failure with them is not that high. In no-limit, these are the hands you'll go broke with if you play them against A-K or A-A. To avoid this peril, learn how to fold even good aces.

3. **Respect Raises and Reraises.** People get out of line all the time in limit poker because, again, the price of failure is not that high. In no-limit, though, if you find yourself facing a bet and a raise, a raise and a call, or a raise and a reraise, you can be quite certain that participating players have quality hands. Stay out of these fights with all but your very best holdings. Something like J-J, for example, is well worth a raise if no one else has opened, but if there's a flurry of bets, raises, and calls before the action gets to you, those jacks must go in the muck.

4. **Be Prepared to Bluff.** Some players pride themselves on "never getting out of line." In no-limit, you have to get out of line from time to time, just to win your share of uncontested flops. Regardless of your cards, for example, be ready to attack the blinds by raising unopened pots in late position. Players who can't bluff give away too much edge in no-limit.

5. **Be Prepared to Call.** Not every bet or raise signifies a real hand, and if you don't call 'em down from time to time,

they'll just run all over you. It takes real courage to call someone you *hope* is bluffing, but successfully snapping off a bluff is almost as emotionally rewarding (and every cent as financially rewarding) as successfully running one.

6. **Be Aware of the Odds.** In limit poker, the pots often get so large that it's correct to call one more bet with even the slimmest chance of winning. Not so in no-limit. If you're contemplating calling a big bet, you need to know that you'll get sufficient return on your investment if you hit your hand. Practice keeping track of the pot size in hands you don't play so that you'll know where you're at in the heat of real battle.

7. **Set Traps.** Sometimes when you have a big hand you're better off not betting it. Check, then check again, and maybe someone will be emboldened enough to make a big bluff at the pot. Remember that whole stacks are at stake. With well-concealed monster holdings, your goal should be to capture every chip you can.

8. **Beware of Traps.** You're not the only one tricky enough to trap, nor can you always avoid falling into them. If someone check-raises you for a huge amount of chips, bear in mind that they're much more likely to be check-raise trapping than check-raise bluffing. If discretion is the better part of valor, be prepared to do the brave thing and flee.

9. **Keep Caring About the Money.** If you're running badly in a no-limit cash game, it's easy to stop caring about how many buy-ins you've put into the game. It's also easy to get desperate about getting even. Both of these leaks in your game will cost you much, much more in no-limit than in limit poker. When you find yourself past the point of pain, you've got to get out of the game.

10. **Take Your Time.** A tip so nice I had to list it twice. Rushing is death in no-limit. Treat every decision as a puzzle to be solved, and take the time to solve the puzzle properly. You might discover an overlooked piece of information, but in any case, you won't fall victim to your own impetuosity.

14

GETTING SERIOUS ABOUT YOUR GAME

♠

Big Al Fresco plays poker in a home game every third Thursday from 7 P.M. until midnight. Al thinks hard about his poker—every third Thursday from 7 P.M. until midnight. The rest of the time he occupies his mind with other things: his job; his relationships; his interest in the Restoration comedies of William Congreve. Al enjoys poker, and I honestly don't know why he doesn't spend more time thinking about his game. Maybe he sees no room for improvement, and so no need for study. Maybe he just doesn't get his jollies that way. I don't think he's lazy; perhaps he hasn't gone far enough into poker to realize how much farther he could go.

Smooth Jack Lowe plays in the same third Thursday game, but he thinks about poker all the time. He has a fervor for poker and a burning desire to evolve and grow in the game. Using his home game as a base, he has lately started making forays into local card-rooms and games online. He doesn't expect to turn pro any time soon—doesn't really want to—but he does expect poker to be a self-funding hobby. He wants to be a net-plus player, and to that end he devotes serious energy to exploring and expanding his poker horizons.

At some point everyone who plays poker reaches the Al and Jack crossroad, where they decide whether they want poker to be a fixed focus of their attention or just another star in their galaxy of interests. For some it's not a choice. They're simply swept away by their passion for the game and find themselves committed to mastering it almost before they know they're even into it. For others, well, they dabble and move on. That's okay. Poker's not for everyone, and far be it from me to claim that it's as essential to the human experience as, say, the Restoration comedies of William Congreve. If you're one of those, though, who want to establish and grow a practice of poker, there are certain solid steps you can take.

Track Your Results. The line of demarcation between the casual player and the dedicated poker enthusiast is simple and clear: *Serious players keep score.* They record in a notebook or spreadsheet the net result of all their poker sessions. They never lie. They never "forget" to record a big loss, no matter how much the loss may sting, because they know that the bottom line isn't nearly so important as the willingness to face their outcomes honestly. Win or lose, they're determined to know where they stand.

Many—perhaps most—players would rather not know where they stand. They'd just as soon not face the painful truth of a losing session. They prefer to rely on "anecdotal memory," the fuzziness of which allows them to claim, "Well, I about broke even; I guess I usually do." This is *gamnesia*, a trick of the mind that lets gamblers remember their wins and conveniently forget their losses. Needless to say, it's not the pinnacle of intellectual rigor.

Other players don't keep score because they are aware that individual outcomes don't matter. Taking the longest possible view of their poker career, they know that the results of a single session are probably perfectly irrelevant. They also know that the difference between a winning night and a losing night might come down to the turn of a single card, a card they have no control over and in some sense would rather not be beholden to. I have no problem with this thinking. It's good to detach from outcomes and it's great to take the long view. The point of keeping records, though, is not to feel good or bad about wins or losses, but to have a means of analyzing our performance so that we can identify and plug holes in our game. Consider the case of Les Ismor.

Les plays in two different weekly home games, one at his house and one across town. He started recording his results in both games about six months ago, and steadfastly ignored those results until he'd accumulated enough numbers to feel confident that short-term fluctuation had given way to legitimate trends. Recently, Les gave those numbers a good, hard look and found a curious thing. Though the stakes were the same and many of the players were the same in both games, he almost always booked wins in the "away" game, but couldn't seem to come out ahead at home. This puzzled Les, and it took him a while to locate the leak. Can you guess what it is?

Les is a responsible citizen. He doesn't drink when he plays across town because he knows he has to drive home later. When he hosts at home, there's no such constraint and over time Les had allowed himself to indulge in the odd schnapps or six. Although it gave him a buzz, the booze hurt his concentration, a fact reflected in his performance. Faced with the evidence of this, he decided to stop "throwing the party" and went back to just hosting the game.

Your rigorous records will reveal a trove of useful information about your play. Do you perform well in short sessions but lose your focus as the hours grow long? Are you a nonsmoker whose play degrades in a smoke-filled room? Can you score big in card-rooms where your starting requirements are rigid but not in home games where you let yourself go loose? Do you play scared when the money's too big but careless when the money's too small? All the answers will be there in your accumulated data, if you're will-ing to collect it faithfully and interpret it honestly.

This needn't be a complex task. There's purpose-built software like *StatKing* or *Card Player Analyst* that can store and sort your results, but at the end of the day you don't need much more than a simple chart like this.

Date	Location	Duration	Game	Limit	Net	Notes
10/12/1492	Vespucci's home game	5 hours	Dealer's choice	$3-6	($125)	Stay away from 7-27
12/7/1941	Club Tora Tora Tora	2 hours	Hold'em	$5-10	$200	Good, aggressive play

How, or how extensively, you keep records is not as important as the fact of keeping them in the first place. Your commitment to tracking your results tells the world (and concerned family or friends) that you're serious-minded about your poker, that you play to win, and that if you *don't* win, you'll damn well know the reason why. Not that you have to book a win every poker night. Your own records will quickly show you that that can't happen. Doesn't matter. If you have an active and thoughtful practice of poker, your results will trend positive over time.

Have a Bankroll. A common concern for tyro poker players is *bankroll.* How much do you need? Where do you get it and what if you lose it? How is it managed? What can be done to keep it from trickling out? If you're playing $5 buy-in games where swings of so much as a sawbuck are rare, this isn't really an issue, for you can get an adequate bankroll at the nearest ATM. But as soon as you move up to meaningful numbers (and I consider anything with three digits to the left of the decimal place meaningful), you need to think about how to establish and handle your bankroll.

The first thing you want to do is acknowledge that *poker money is not like other money.* It does one thing and one thing only: It plays poker. Physical separation is the key. Have two wallets (or purses or thick rubber bands): one for your everyday money and one for poker money. This physical separation will help with psychological separation, your declaration to yourself and the world that poker money is sacrosanct, not to be poached for the odd tank of gas or café latte, and not to be squandered on such frivolities as food, clothing, and shelter. Once you move some cash off to the side and say to yourself, *That's for poker only,* you'll see both the money and yourself in a different light. The money is a player's bankroll; therefore, *you* are a *player*.

You can seed your initial bankroll from a variety of sources: birthday money; the change jar on your dresser; windfalls such as an inheritance; or, you know, that liquor store heist you pulled. You can tithe from your income, like a Christmas Club account. You might even just write a check, saying to yourself, *This is my bankroll to start. I'm going to see how big I can build it, how long I can make it last.*

Once you've got your bankroll rolling, your goal is to keep it alive—growing if possible, but at minimum alive. To that end, you always want to keep in mind the relationship between the size of your bankroll and the size of the game you're playing, so that you don't risk too much of it at any one time. A thousand-dollar bankroll will adequately fund play at a $2–4 limit, but would never survive at $20–40, where, with nothing more than normal fluctuation, you'd quickly find yourself tapped out.

The higher the ratio between your bankroll and your bets, then, the safer your bankroll will be. As your bankroll gets bigger, you can move up to successively larger games. Just don't let your ambition or your ego put you out ahead of your funding. Also recognize that it's easier to replace a small bankroll than a large one (from money found in the wash, for example, or the aforementioned liquor store heist). You should be prepared to take bigger chances with your smaller bankroll and smaller chances with your bigger one. But don't worry too much if you lose your bankroll entirely. It happens to everyone sooner or later, professional player and avid amateur alike. This is why we establish a separate bankroll in the first place. This is also why we say, "Bet with your head, not over it." You'll find it emotionally easier to deal with the loss of your poker money if it's not the loss of large sums of vital household money as well.

If you find yourself replenishing or rebuilding your bankroll too frequently, you need to go looking for leaks. It may be, for example, that you're not quite as skilled as you think you are. (Your performance records will shed light on this.) Some especially bad players have simply retired from poker because their abilities were not up to the challenge of making their bankroll last. A second major cause of leaks is playing too big for one's bankroll. If you're routinely "bottoming out" your bankroll, drop down to a level where your bankroll can last. Remember that success in this case means nothing more than keeping your bankroll alive. The purpose of being in action, to put it rather strangely, is just to keep you in action.

If you're playing with skill and discipline in games of appropriate size and you still can't seem to sustain your bankroll, ask yourself where else your poker money is going. Many players treat their poker bankroll as a "general gaming" bankroll as well. They use money from poker to fund everything from office pools to lottery tickets to slot machines. Don't do this. Draw a clear distinction between poker and your other betting recreations. As we know, poker is one game of chance where your decisions matter. You may feel you have a system for beating the slot machines (chanting *Hari Krishna*, for example, before every handle pull), but the fact is that those are outcomes you can't control, not like you can manipulate the size of a poker pot or the way your opponents view their chances of winning the hand. If you want to play mindless, negative expectation "games of chance," go right ahead. Just don't place your bets from your poker bankroll or soon you will have no poker bankroll left.

People have strong emotional relationships to money. This should not surprise us, for in this modern world, money equals survival. If you fixate too strongly, though, on the money/survival equation, you end up playing scared all the time, and scared poker is not likely to be winning poker. Having a poker bankroll separate from your other money disconnects you from this strong emotional tie and allows you to play your best.

Don't go crazy. Hardly a day passes these days that you don't see a poker broadcast on television or a poker story in the local press. New poker magazines are springing up like weeds. Poker books proliferate, with this one doing gleefully nothing to stem *that* tide.

Search the word *poker* on the internet and you'll get more than ten million hits. Or anyway I did, and that's four million more than I got for baseball, so now you tell me what the national pastime is. Even five years ago it would have been impossible to imagine this explosion in poker information—*poker porn* we call it, because when we encounter it, it makes us want to do nothing so much as *go play poker.*

No doubt about it, poker is a very compelling game. The problem-solving challenge plus the adrenaline rush of risking real money add up to a heady cocktail, a cocktail too heady for some. I'm happy to fan the flames of your poker desire, but I must also remind you (while indeed reminding myself) that the trouble with *too far* is you never know you're going till you've gone.

Poker is especially compelling when you're new to the game and your learning curve is steep. The brave new world of position raises and isolation bluffs can leave you dizzy with contemplation and eager to find a game right now where you can put your new chops to the test. Left unchecked, poker, like gas, will expand to fill the available space in your life. I'm sure you're not opposed to that—you'd hardly have come this far in this book if you were averse to the advice: "Play more poker!"

However, you're not the only one in your life. Your new passion for poker has to come at the expense of something, perhaps your former passion for the Restoration comedies of William Congreve, and it must necessarily impact those around you: your spouse, family, friends, dog, or fellow Congreve-heads. At best they'll feel jealous of the attention they've lost. At worst, they'll worry that you're falling into a sinkhole of obsession and start leaving Gamblers Anonymous brochures in your mailbox. To allay their fears, not forgetting that their fears may be at least a little legitimate, there are three things you can do.

First, *strike a balance.* "Moderation in all things," counseled Terence, and he was smart about such stuff, having also said, "Fortune helps the brave," and, "Too much liberty corrupts us all." Terence predates poker night by a good two thousand years, but if he were around to counsel us now, I'm sure he would suggest that we make poker an important part of our life—even a vital part of our life—just not *all* our life. Especially if we think we have skills in this area, we run the real risk of going completely overboard. Every time we *don't* play, we tell ourselves, we're leaving money lying on the table, and how can that be good? Remember, money's only important to people with nothing important in their lives. Put your poker in the context of a well-balanced life experience and your enthusiasm for the game will reward you with endless pleasure for as long as you live.

Second, *demonstrate your balance.* Keep doing the other things you love in your life, with the other people you love in your life. Make those around you aware that, while you have every intention of being the most kick-ass poker player you can be, it won't come at the expense of your relationships, your health, your sanity, or your spiritual well-being. And yes, it's possible to be a spiritual poker player, above and beyond, *Oh, God, please let me get an ace right now!* The truth, as they say, is revealed under pressure, and the sublime pressures of poker will reveal truths of your character that you never imagined were there. Along those lines, it wouldn't hurt to teach poker to your surrounding doubting Thomases, so they can see for themselves what good, clean fun—and useful revelations—it provides.

Third, *open your books.* Keep records, and be willing to show those records to people who have a legitimate interest. If you're running net-plus, this will relieve them of their concern that you're heading for a new home in a refrigerator box. If you're not running net-plus, but your losses are manageable, this is a subject that can be addressed openly and honestly. And if your losses aren't manageable, then you may need to curb your enthusiasm for poker, either by limiting the time you spend on it or the money you invest in it. The bottom line is, well, the bottom line. There's no excuse for anything less than total honesty here.

True story: I was at LA's Bicycle Casino one night and I happened to be in the men's room, where a guy was talking on his cell phone behind a stall door. "Right *now?*" he says defensively. "Right now I'm at Home Depot!" Poor sucker. I don't know if he was lying to his wife, mother, boss, or dog, but the fact of his lying must certainly have killed his enjoyment of the game. Don't be that guy. It's fine to love poker; just don't love it at the expense of your healthy and balanced life, or, ever, at the expense of the truth.

Set rational goals. After a lifetime of poker nights, I find that my goals for the game are the same as they were when I first sat down.

1. Have fun.
2. Play my best.
3. Try to take out more money than I put in.

Those are reasonable goals, and I encourage you to adopt them as your own.

However . . .

Everyone who's ever been bitten by the poker bug encounters a moment like this: *Hey, I killed 'em last night. Five hundred bucks in four hours! If I played like that all the time, I could pull down a serious chunk of change!* Dreams of poker riches are not uncommon among poker players, even home poker players, but like the man said, "Playing poker is a hard way to make an easy living." How hard? Let's look.

Suppose you figure you need to earn $60,000 a year to live a decent life. It's generally accepted that an expert poker player can win one and a half big bets per hour. If you're prepared to play 40 hours a week, then you've got 2,000 poker playing hours at your disposal this year. (I'm giving you two weeks off for vacation, aren't I nice?) Just find yourself a soft little $10–20 poker game and start taking out $30 an hour. Two thousand hours later, you've got your $60K, right? Of course, there is the small matter of fluctuation. You may have killed your home game twice in a row, but you won't kill every game every time. To feel well-funded in a $10–20 poker game, you'll need at least $5,000 in ready cash. And that's cash you can't touch. You can't pay your bills out of that, or fix your car, or even buy a baseball cap to pull down low over your eyes when you play. Start drawing money out of your bankroll and it won't be big enough to sustain you at $10–20. You'll have to drop down to $5–10—but where are you going to find 80 hours a week to play poker?

So your $5,000 in ready cash really needs to be something like $10,000, and at that you'd be at the low edge of what most pros consider a reasonable professional player's bank. And I gotta ask you: If you have ten grand in ready cash available, don't you think you could put it to work in a more profitable venue than a poker game? You could start a business, buy a store of some kind—just not one of those liquor stores that people keep robbing—or invest in your education.

Still, every day men and women in all walks of life decide to chuck it all and take their shot. They like the idea of freedom, of being their own boss. The ones who succeed have passion, courage, smarts, talent, discipline, and an adequate bankroll. The ones who fail . . . are most of them. I know it's a long way down the road—you may never even have *played* poker before reading this book—but if you ever decide that a poker cowboy's life is the life for you, let me make this modest proposal: Serve an apprenticeship first. Set yourself the goal of becoming a pro in five years' time. During those five years, keep your day job, and play as much serious poker as your time and your bankroll allow. Now here comes the important part: Take all of your profit, above and beyond what you need to sustain your bankroll, and put it into your "poker independence fund." Don't fix the car out of that money and don't buy baseball caps to pull down over your eyes. Just set it aside. When your apprenticeship is up, if there's no money in the cookie jar, you'll know you're not ready to turn pro. If you've made some serious coin, you'll be able to demonstrate to yourself and to those who care about you that this is a job you can do. You'll also have the bankroll you need to do the job for real.

Of course, before you win the World Series of Poker, or even set up shop as Lord of the Local Cardroom, you're going to have to make the transition from home poker to public poker. Let's tackle that subject next.

15

FROM POKER NIGHT TO CASINOS AND BEYOND

♠

Having come this far in your poker progress, you might now be thinking about venturing into the public poker arena. It may be that your home game companions have gotten a little silly for your taste: "A guy walks into a bar . . . *Ouch!*" It may be that you've outgrown the stakes: "No, I *don't* have change for a dime." It may be that you're ready to challenge yourself at a higher level: "If I can make it here, I can make it anywhere!" Or it may simply be that you want to play poker more frequently than your weekly or monthly poker night allows. Good news. Public poker awaits. Bad news. It's *scary.*

♦ ♦ ♦ **Breaking In**

Even if you're a seasoned home game player, your first foray into a public cardroom can be more than a little intimidating. Where your home game is self-dealt, here they have professional dealers.

Where your home game is dealer's choice, here they have given games at fixed limits. Where the rules in your home game may be no more formal than "What I say goes," here they have a long list of posted procedures. Where the guys in your home game all know one another as friends, colleagues, and coworkers, this is a room full of strangers, and every one seems like a lean, mean poker machine. You feel a little like a sheep sandwich at the Wolves' Club luncheon.

But not for long.

Poker rooms in America can generally be found either as stand-alone establishments, as in California, Washington, and Montana, or housed in casinos, as in Nevada, Mississippi, Atlantic City, and elsewhere. The only difference between the two is that with card-rooms in casinos, you have to run a certain gauntlet of slot machines and table games to reach your poker haven. And here let me step aside for a moment and speak to those of you who have experience with casino games like craps, blackjack, and roulette: Once you play poker in a casino, you'll probably never play those other games again. Here's why.

When you play craps, you play against the house. When you play blackjack, you play against the house. When you play baccarat, slots, video poker, keno, big wheel, or flip-it, you play against the house. And we all know that the house has an edge. As they say, "If you could beat Vegas, Vegas wouldn't be there." But when you play poker, you don't play against the house. They take their rake, of course, but the joust is strictly between you and other people. People—believe it or not—just like you.

I know what you're thinking: *They're* not *like me. They're experts, they're pros.* Not true! Sure, some folks you meet in public cardrooms are trying to make their living at the game, but the vast majority are people who have figured out that sitting at a poker table is more fun than standing at a craps table, plus you get to sit down. Some of them are very smart players, but some are not very smart at all. They only seem smart because they're already there. They joke with the dealers. The slang of poker falls trippingly from their tongues. They shuffle their chips with practiced ease. In short, they know the game.

But they didn't always know the game. They started exactly where we all start: by taking that first step over the threshold. Where you are, they have been; where they are, you will be. Though they seem to be vastly more knowledgeable, skilled, and confident than you could ever hope to be, that's really only an illusion based on experience, experience you can easily acquire for yourself.

That's what makes poker the game to play in casinos. Since you're not playing against the house, you have a real chance to win money from people who are more or less exactly like you. And believe me, the thrill of winning money from a fellow gladiator in the public poker arena makes the thrill of beating the boys in your home game pale by comparison.

I know, I know . . . you're still worried about the first time. You're worried that your raw inexperience will show, that they'll laugh at you and you'll feel a fool. Well, you may feel a fool, but they certainly won't laugh. To the contrary, they'll do everything in their power to make you feel welcome in the game. Not out of the goodness of their hearts, of course: By making you feel comfortable and relaxed, they hope to win your money. But you can surprise them by holding your own from the start, if you just do one thing: The first time you go to play in a public cardroom, *don't play at all!*

Keeping your money safely in your pocket (or locked in the glove compartment of your car), just walk in and look around.

Don't feel self-conscious. No one will bother you. No one will challenge you. Probably no one will notice you. That neon sign floating above you, flashing, POKER VIRGIN! POKER VIRGIN! that's all in your head. No one can see that but you.

Check out the tables. Each one will have a little brass or plastic placard, usually located to the left or the right of the dealer, denoting the game being played and the betting structure. You might encounter one, for example, that says $2–4 TEXAS HOLD'EM. It will also list the amount of the blinds and the maximum house rake.

Somewhere in the room you'll find a sign listing all of the house rules. Spend a few moments in solemn communion with this sign. It will tell you such things as the minimum buy-ins at the various tables, the number of raises permitted per betting round (usually three, just like in your home game), whether the house allows proposition (house-paid) players, terms and conditions of the jackpot, if any, and so on. If you read something you don't understand, just go up to anyone who works there and ask for an explanation. Since you're not playing today, there's no harm in blowing your newbie cover. When you come back next time, you probably won't see many (or any) of the same faces anyhow.

Stop by the sign-up desk. There you'll find either a white board or a sheet of paper listing all the different games and different limits being spread at the time. Were you ready to play, you would give your name or initials to the person working there, and he'd put you on the waiting list for the game or games of your choice. But, really, don't plan on playing the first time. You're in an alien environment, and no matter how comfortable you come to feel during your first foray, you'll feel ten times more comfortable on your next visit. You'll also feel terrific about the discipline you showed by resisting the urge (an urge I promise you will feel) to dive into deep water. Spend your time this time just watching.

Find a game you like at a limit you like and camp out on it for a while. Note the procedures of the game: how the players post their antes or blinds and bets; how they act in turn; how the dealer runs the show. Note also the sort of hands people play and the sort of hands they show down. Use your ghosting skills to project yourself into the action.

One thing you find may surprise you: *People play bad!* Now that you know how to choose your starting hands with care and to bet with the best of it, you'll be shocked to discover how many players don't seem to have grasped the knack of that. They call too much, they chase too much, they're just generally passive and weak and loose. You don't have to take my word on this. You'll see it for yourself.

And this is the point of the exercise. By encountering card-room poker for the first time as an observer rather than a partici-pant, you'll give yourself the chance to see that the competition is not nearly so fierce as you fear. Yes, there are foes out there with superior cunning and skill—and part of your success will come from recognizing and evading these sharks—but the vast majority of players are not that different from those you face on poker night. You'll have this revelation, I promise: *I can take these guys!*

Now take what you've learned and walk away. Go home and think about poker as you now know it to be played in public. Put together your bankroll, schedule your session, then go back and take your shot. Breeze into the cardroom. Sign up for the game of your choice. Wait till your name is called. Let the floorman show you to your seat. Get chips from the chip runner. Nod with solemn assurance when the dealer asks if you're ready to play.

Then fasten your seatbelt, 'cause the roller-coaster ride is about to start!

Despite your careful preparation and your measured easing in, you *will* be nervous and you *will* be scared. You'll sweat in places you didn't know you could sweat. (For me it was the bottom of my feet.) You'll be awkward with your cards and clumsy with your chips. Your hands will shake and you'll make mistakes— process mistakes, betting mistakes, errors in judgment—but that's to be expected. It's all to be expected. If the money itself isn't enough to kick you into adrenaline shock, the strangeness of it all—the startling fact of your presence in this brave new world— will. Let it wash over you. It's called the buzz of public poker, and it will be with you, in one form or another, for as long as you make these cardrooms your home-away-from-home-game.

The first time you bluff out a stranger, you'll feel like a spy. The first time they push you a pot, you'll feel like a lion. The first time you quit winners, you'll feel like the king of the world. The first time you *rack off* (lose every chip in your rack) you'll feel— well, you'll find out what that's like. You'll find out what it's all like, and you'll find out rather quickly. By your second or third session, you'll forget that the cardroom ever seemed foreign or foreboding. Before you know it, you'll be a chip-shuffling, slang-slinging regular, and when you see some doe-eyed first-timer wander into the room, you'll think to yourself, *That hapless newbie, he doesn't know the ropes. Hmm . . . how can I get him into my game?*

♦ ♦ ♦ Strategy Adjustments

Be Rested and Ready. The most important thing to remember in moving from poker night to public poker is that you're no longer playing with friends. You're playing with strangers and they're serious about taking your money. In home games, where people are horsing around and playing for fun, you can get away with some inattention or carelessness. In the cardrooms, with both experienced competition and the house rake to overcome, you can't afford to be sloppy or self-indulgent—*ever*. Every chip matters and every bet counts. It's vital, then, that you come to the club rested and relaxed and ready to deliver the toughest, most disciplined game you've got. If you're not prepared to play your best, just skip it until you are.

Set a Time Limit and a Loss Limit. Home games always end at a certain time. You start at 7 P.M., say, and deal off at midnight. In the cardrooms, players come and go, but the game goes on and on. You get caught up in the action, the hours fly by, and soon you find yourself playing longer, perhaps much longer, than you ever play at home. You don't feel tired—you're pumped on the buzz—but fatigue sets in, judgment goes south, and the next thing you know your chips are gone. To combat this problem, give yourself an exit strategy. Plan to leave at a certain time, and then stick to that plan. It's also useful to set yourself a loss limit, a budget you can stick to. Don't set a win limit. If you're playing well, keep playing—until you reach your time limit, then pack up your profit and go.

Play Extra Tight at First. During your first few sessions, or during the start of any session, it's a good idea to *play tighter than usual, even unnaturally tight*. You'll be facing at least some unknown opponents nearly every time you sit down to play, and you'll want to observe them closely. Get to know their strengths and weaknesses and their approach to the game. Who's straightforward? Who's tricky? Who's disciplined? Who's on tilt? These are questions you'll want to answer before you start contesting a lot of pots.

Each home game, after all, is pretty much a continuation of the last and a prelude to the next, but each cardroom session is its own party with a different list of invited guests. Make sure you get to know them well before you start to dance.

Choose the Right Game. *Game selection* is never an issue on poker night. You're pretty much stuck with that slate of players. In cardrooms, though, you'll often find that you have the choice of two or more different tables spreading the game you want to play at limits you like. Sometimes one game will be markedly better than the other, and by better we mean easier to beat, filled with more of those soft, loose, predictable opponents we love so well. If you find yourself in a game that's not so good—one with tough, tricky or hyperaggressive enemies—shop around for a more profitable situation. Tell the floorman that you want a table change and jump to a better game as soon as a seat comes open.

It's not always possible to tell at a glance whether a game is good or not, but here's a quickie method for making an educated guess. First, contemplate how much money you feel comfortable putting on the table, for instance a rack of 100 $1 chips in a $3–6 game. Then look at the game you're thinking of entering and count the chips that each player has. If the table average is at or about your $100 buy-in, you can feel confident that your Big Ben will sufficiently equip you to do battle here. But if you see several players with several racks of chips in front of them, this tells you that they're currently dominating the game, and may very well dominate you, too. Even if they're only just catching lucky right now, they're likely to be inspired by winning and therefore playing their best. Plus, they have a lot more chips than you, which means they can push you around. Don't mess with them. Go find a game where the stack sizes are more in keeping with your intended buy-in. It's the worst kind of self-indulgent self-destruction to get into a game you know to be unpromising, just because you'd rather be in action than not.

Choose the Right Seat. *Seat selection* is likewise not often a consideration in home games. Everyone has their favorite seat and they pretty much stick to them week after week. Butch sits by the window 'cause smoke drives him crazy. Cole likes to be close to the kitchen. Frank wants to see the TV. Jesse sits facing the door because that's what Wild Bill Hickok should have done. In cardrooms, unlike home games, you can change seats any time one opens up at your table. If you find that there's one particularly strong player in your game, look for an opportunity to *sit to that player's left*, so that you can act after him and decide, based on his actions, whether you want to mix it up with him or not.

Much can be said on the subject of seat selection, but what it all boils down to is this: Whenever possible, *try to put strong, unpredictable players on your right and loose, passive ones on your left*. In this way you gain position over the foes who threaten you most and cede position to those who threaten you least. (You can adopt this thinking for your home games as well, assuming you can move Butch away from the window.)

Manage Your Image. *Image play* takes on a different quality in cardrooms. Back home where everyone knows you, your image plays are more or less variations on a theme: crankier than usual, loopier than usual, what have you. In cardrooms, you're generally unknown to your foes, which means that you can do more with your image, since your image, at least for a while, is all they'll have to go on. Early in your cardroom career, for instance, you have a natural "innocent" image working for you. Wed that perceived innocence to a strong, selective game plan and you'll have people paying you off with worse hands all night. Soon enough, though, you'll lose your innocence, and thus your innocent image. At that point you'll have to shift to something else: crazy or careless or bitchy or whatever works for you. It really doesn't matter what image you adopt, so long as you make some effort to *create a gap between how you play and how you appear to play*. Not only will this add an element of deception to your game, it will further focus your attention on the nuances of public poker.

Look for Tells Right Away. Just as the impact of image changes in a public setting, the utility of tells shifts as well. Against foes you see all the time, you discover reliable tells you can regularly exploit. In cardrooms, against opponents you've never seen before and may never see again, it's important to look for *tells in the moment*, tells that can help you make the right decision right now. (Of course, it's important that you guard against giving off tells of your own, but that's true in any game you play.) I can't possibly give you a complete catalog of reliable cardroom tells, but remember the rule of thumb that *players who are weak act strong, and players who are strong act weak*. There's no substitute for really knowing your enemies, though, so be sure to ghost your foes extensively when you're not in the hand, looking for starting requirements, betting patterns, and, of course, tells.

♦ ♦ ♦ Tournaments

Tournament poker is a great way to build your cardroom experience and confidence for a small fixed price. Many cardrooms have regularly scheduled daily or weekly tournaments with buy-ins in the $20 to $50 range. Where you might buy into a cash game for fifty bucks and then spend another fifty and another fifty after that, once you've paid your tournament fee, you've reached your maximum financial exposure. After that, the worst you can do is bust out. And who knows? You might even win the thing.

All players in a poker tournament start with an equal number of chips. You might, for example, get T$1,000 (a thousand dollars in tournament chips) for your $20 buy-in. Note that there's no one-to-one relationship between the money you pay to enter the tournament and the number of chips you get, nor can you redeem your chips for cash any time you like, as you could in a *ring* (cash) game. Once you sit down to play in a tournament, you're there for the duration. Either you'll make it to the money or you'll go broke trying.

Tournaments are played in rounds, usually twenty minutes or half an hour in length. After each round of play, the blinds, antes, and/or betting limits go up. It's the fact of these rising limits that makes tournaments work. With T$1,000, everyone can survive at T$10–20 betting limits, but when the limits get up to T$100–200 or T$200–400, you either build a big stack or find yourself on the rail.

A tournament can last anywhere from a few hours to several *days*, so concentration and stamina are issues of real concern. If you've been banging heads with your tournament foes all day and half the night, it's hard to have your best perception and decision-making skills working for you at the final table—and yet that's when you *must* be thinking clearly, for that's when the decisions you make will matter most in your finishing position and your payoff. It's useful, then, to think of a tournament as a marathon—

a commitment of time and energy that should not be undertaken lightly. Pace yourself. Be well rested, well fed, and ready to play your best from the first hand to the last.

Every player's entry fee goes into the prize pool, and that prize pool is divided among the top tournament finishers. The number of places paid depends on the size of the field, but payouts to the final two tables are typical. The payoff structure is usually weighted heavily in favor of the first-, second-, and third-place finishers, and while it's never bad to finish "in the money," the top three spots should be your destination of choice.

The great thing about tournaments is how much bang for your buck you get. If you did nothing but play supremely tight, you could make your way to, or past, the middle of most tournaments. This will give you a look at a lot of hands and greatly increase the number of cardroom poker hours you've logged. It won't get you to the money, though! For that to happen, you're going to have to get some strong cards or make some strong moves or both. No one wins tournaments, especially big tournaments, without some luck along the way, but also no one wins on luck alone. So when you enter a tournament, especially early in your poker career, think of it as an opportunity to try your luck and work on your skills in a situation where your risk is limited and your reward could be quite great.

Home Tournaments. You can spice up your home games by throwing in a tournament from time to time. For example, you might play your regular cash structure for the first few hours of poker night and then, at a set time, cash everyone out and start over with a short-term tournament. As people bust out, they can either stick around to watch the action or call it a night and go home. Alternatively, if you have enough room for two games and enough players in your poker pool, you can start the evening with a tournament and feed the early bust-outs into a ring game.

Below you'll find a chart showing the betting limits per round in a typical fixed-limit Texas hold'em tournament. This is by no means the only tournament structure you can use, but it's one that will give a reasonable amount of play for a T$1,000 buy-in. You can speed up or slow down a tournament simply by shortening or lengthening the amount of time that each round lasts. As a rule, the shorter the playing rounds, the greater the "luck factor" will be. Fifteen-minute rounds will turn the tournament into a bit of a crap shoot, while half-hour rounds will give players' skill and strategy some room to move.

Home Tournament Structure

Level	Blinds	Limits
1	10/15	15/30
2	15/25	25/50
3	25/50	50/100
4	50/100	100/200
5	100/200	200/400
6	200/400	400/800
7	300/600	600/1200
8	500/1000	1000/2000

**Subsequent Blinds and Limits Double Every
Round Until Tournament Is Complete**

Typical payout for a one-table home tournament is 50 percent to first place, 30 percent to second place, and 20 percent to third place. If you have more players you can pay more places, but keep the money heavy in the top three spots, for, from the smallest poker night tourney to million-dollar megatournaments, there's no point in having the contest if the top prize isn't worth winning.

Satellites. In the biggest tournaments, the top prize is not only worth winning, it can actually change your life. Take down a million-dollar first prize and you'll have what James Clavell called "fuck you money," enough scratch to fund whatever fantasy you harbor in life. Trouble is, the tournaments with the biggest prize pools also have the biggest buy-ins, and plunking down $25,000 to enter the main event at Bellagio's Five-Star World Poker Classic may not be the wisest bankroll investment you can make—or even remotely possible.

Well, that's why God invented satellites.

A satellite is a minitournament, a feeder, if you will, into the big events. Suppose there's a big tournament that you'd like to play in, but don't feel comfortable putting up long green on a long shot. You can enter a satellite instead, for a fraction of the big event's buy-in. If you win the satellite, you've won your buy-in to the main event. If you lose, it's a loss your bankroll can stand.

There are two types of satellites: single-table satellites and supersatellites. In a single-table satellite, also known as a *shootout*, each player puts up roughly 10 percent of the big tournament's buy-in and the winner gets "a ticket to the show." Supersatellites, or *supers*, have larger fields but smaller buy-ins than the shootouts. They play much the same as ordinary multitable, moderate buy-in tournaments, except that the top places are paid in tournament entry fees instead of (or possibly in addition to) cash. If you win the super, and then win the main event, you'll have parlayed a modest investment into a monster payday.

Is such a parlay possible? Just ask Chris Moneymaker, who began his journey to poker immortality with a $40 buy-in satellite on an internet poker site. Winning that satellite got him into the $10,000 no-limit hold'em tournament at the 2003 World Series of Poker . . . which he won, collecting a cool $2.5 million. Talk about bang for your buck!

♦ ♦ ♦ Online Poker

Online cardrooms have the benefit of total anonymity, which makes them a great place to get over your initial self-consciousness and insecurity. So what if you don't quite know what you're doing? To your foes out there in cyberspace, you're not you, you're just *mirplo* or *jellyfish* or whatever other screen name you've selected for yourself. You might make a fool out of yourself, but they'll never know it's you.

Even better, almost every online poker site has the so-called *free play option*, your chance to play on real poker software against real live opponents, but not for real money. Using this option, you can learn everything you need to know about selecting your game and your seat in the game, about buying your chips and posting your blinds. It's the same "break it down into parts" strategy as visiting a cardroom and just observing once without playing, only online you actually get to play while you learn, albeit not for cash. In fact, you don't want to be in any big hurry to put real money into an online poker site. As I point out in my book *Killer Poker Online: Crushing the Internet Game*, there are many pitfalls unique to online poker, and the slower you go, the more of these you'll see coming and sidestep them.

Some people swear by internet poker. They love being able to find action any time they want, 24/7/365, in the privacy of their own home. For those who live in cardroom-poor areas of the world (Utah and Kiribati come to mind), online poker is the only supplement to poker night they have, short of jaunts to Las Vegas (easy from Utah, a schlep from Kiribati). Those with short attention spans find online poker a paradise where they can play two, three, four, or more games at the same time. Others like the fact that no one can see them, and therefore can't possibly pick off tells.

But online poker isn't just a computerized version of live play. It's a whole 'nother thing. Consider some of these unique properties of online poker.

Speed of Play. With Seth having to have the game explained five times and Aaron forgetting that it's his turn to bet *again*, and Andy off in the bathroom, home games are lucky if they get in fifteen hands per hour. Cardrooms look to turn the deck over thirty times or more, and they're happy to do so because the more hands they deal, the more rake they collect. Online, you might see sixty to a hundred hands an hour—even more if you find yourself at a short-handed table. Naturally this requires you to make quick, and possibly rash, decisions, but that's only half the problem. The accelerated pace of play has the inevitable effect of *magnifying your errors*. If you like to chase long shots, to take one example, you'll be punished for this hole in your game four or five or six times faster than you would be in a home game. Yikes! Online poker can give new meaning to the phrase "going broke in a hurry."

Lack of Visual Information. One of your home game stalwarts makes a big bet. You try to look him in the eye, but he won't meet your gaze. You figure if he were bluffing, he'd try to stare you down, so he probably wants you to call. You fold. Disappointed, he turns over his four of a kind, and you feel vindicated in your ability to read your foe. Online, you'll never have this opportunity. There are no eyes to look into, no gazes to meet, no shaky hands or sweaty palms to note. All you have to go on is the situation at hand and any prior experience you may have had against a given foe. If you're the sort of person who gets a lot of tells and clues and cues from your real-world poker foes, the internet version of the game will give you fits.

Wealth of Statistical Information. What online poker loses in terms of tells it more than makes up for in raw numbers. Most internet sites will provide you with *hand histories*, detailed records of hundreds or thousands of hands that you or your opponents have played. A close examination of these hand histories will reveal some interesting trends and tendencies about your foes, and you can definitely sharpen your own game by analyzing your past performance and seeing where you went right or wrong. Plus you can keep unlimited written notes about every foe you face, something you definitely can't do in live games. How useful would it be to know that a player betting into you has *never bluffed before* for as long as you've watched him play? The opportunity to handicap your opponents in this way may very well make the lack of visual tells irrelevant, but you've got to be dedicated enough to gather all this the data and then deft enough to use it.

The "Virtual" Environment. When you're playing poker in a home game or a cardroom, there's no doubt in your mind about where you are. You're in a poker setting, and everything in your environment confirms that fact. When you're playing online, though, you may be sitting at the same desk you use for paying bills, surfing the web, (writing a book!), or dozens of other everyday activities. It's hard to think of this space as a poker room—and dismayingly easy to forget that you're playing real poker for real money against real foes. The mind may wander, and that's not likely to improve the quality of your poker-related decisions. Nor can you necessarily eliminate normal household distractions like the telephone, a knock at the door, or your dog's urgent need to *go out now!* Keeping your head in the game is a constant challenge when the game is nothing more than a few flat inches of display on your computer screen.

Cashing In and Cashing Out. Buying into your home game is easy. You just lay your money down. Cashing out is easy, too. You count down your chips, collect your dough, and go. Online, getting money into the game involves the transfer of funds from your credit card or bank account to an online poker site, either directly or through an intermediary like NetTeller.com or FirePay.com. There's time and possibly expense involved. Cashing out is even more difficult, not because the sites won't pay you your money—they will—but because of your own psychological resistance to taking money out of action. If you like playing online, you'll want to keep your money right there on the site. Should you then hit a losing streak and go broke, you'll have nothing to show for your investment but the time you got to play.

Collusion. While more is made of this issue than I think is justified, the fact remains that some of your foes *could* be in cahoots with one another. *Revolver23* and *DeputyDawg* might seem to be unrelated strangers at your virtual table, but they could be together in the same room somewhere, or even be the same person logging in on two different computers. If collusion does happen, it's more likely to happen at the higher betting limits, where the payoff will be worth the effort. For this reason, among others, I think it's a good idea to "play small" online. You're less likely to run into nefarious cheaters, and if you should happen to lose your money (even if only through bad luck or bad play), at least it won't be so huge a sum as to materially impact your life in a negative way.

♠ ♠ ♠

Well, there you have it: live action in cardrooms; tournament poker; poker on the internet. If that doesn't meet your poker needs, you're even more obsessive than I am—and I've always considered myself pretty much the head of that class. While it's true that Terence said, "Moderation in all things," Oscar Wilde said, "The only way to get rid of a temptation is to yield to it," and someone else (I think it was me) said, "Anything that's worth doing is worth overdoing," so you can judge for yourself.

16

GRABS AND FAQs

♠

In this chapter, we'll look at some quick tips for improving your play—I call them *grabs*—and also at some frequently asked questions about home poker.

♦ ♦ ♦ Grabs

The first and most important grab I can give you is: *Hey, collect your own grabs!* Every home game has its eccentricities and its unique targets of opportunity, and the original discoveries you make and hoard about your particular poker night will help you more than anything you might cop from me. In some home games, for instance, they play *last round double*, meaning that the betting limits are doubled during the last lap around the table before quitting time. If you know that *everyone* will play *anything* during that time (because, gosh, it's almost time to go back to Pacoima), you'll want to screw down your own starting requirements but, if the opportunity presents itself, really sock it to those who play too loose. Or perhaps you have observed that your pal Joaquin Wounded is a tiger when the night is young but loses focus as the hours go by. Now you know to evade him early and attack him late.

So establish a poker notebook and record your discoveries there. If nothing else, this will set you apart from the players in your game who give no thought to the game from one poker night to the next. Soon you'll have your own favorite grabs. In the meantime, here are some of mine.

Turn Off the Radio. It's poker night and you're driving to the game. You're in a good mood—you're always in a good mood on poker night—and you enhance the mood by cranking up the car stereo and singing along with Sinatra or Springsteen or whoever gets your toes a-tappin'. Recalling that we're interested in thinking our game, not feeling our game, may I suggest that you turn off the radio and let silence descend? Think about the game ahead. Review the known tells and tendencies of the players you'll face tonight. Be aware of your own pitfalls and give yourself articulate cautions against them. I routinely remind myself, for instance, to "start slow." The games I play in always get great as the hour gets late. If I start slow, looking for modest targets of opportunity, I can build momentum and set up the sort of shank-of-the-evening blitzkrieg that my home game foes have come to know and loathe and fear. On the other hand, if I try to do too much too soon, I risk digging myself an emotional and financial hole it'll take me all night to dig out of. I don't play well in a glower. I don't know too many people who do.

Drive time, then, is pep talk time and game plan time. There'll be plenty of opportunity on the way home to sing along with Bruce and feel good about how well you've done.

Or no, actually, turn off the radio then, too. Review the plays you've made and new discoveries you've made. The radio can wait. There's still learning to be done, after all, and the next poker night is never far away.

Go Slow with Games You Don't Know. Every now and then you'll run into a poker variation—an import or invention—that you've never played before. Consider these encounters to be the "Here be dragons" part of your poker map, and proceed with caution. When you don't know a game, there are *many* things you don't know: what's a good starting hand; how big the pots typically get; whether people chase; how big a hand it takes to win; whether there are bluff/steal opportunities; and so on. Even if you think you comprehend the game, even if you've heard and understood when the dealer said, "You must use three cards from your hand and two from the board, stand on one leg when you bet, and re-cite the Gettysburg Address when you declare," that's an awful lot of information to hold on to and process all at once, and you're bound to make mistakes.

Let others make them instead.

Do your learning at their expense.

Fold quietly, then sit quietly and watch. Even if you acquire nothing more than a vague feel for the game, you'll avoid the trap of trying to *play* the game and *learn* the game at the same time. Recognize that the dealer who called the game has a head start— a knowledge head start—over you. And we know how we feel about those.

This advice goes double—triple, *quadruple!*—when you find yourself sitting in for the first time in a new home game, against players unknown to you. You're a stranger in their midst. They know each other; they know the rhythm and texture of their game. They only have to solve *one* of you, but you have to solve *all* of them. That's gonna take some time—time *much* better spent attentively watching than recklessly playing. Even if they're playing poker varieties you know very well, they're playing with their own style and slant. Who plays too loose? Who plays too tight? Who bluffs? Who chases? Who can you put on tilt? Who looks like a threat? Jump into the action without taking the time to figure these things out and you're just flying blind. See that mountain up ahead? Oh, no?

Fold a *lot* early on, and go to school on your new best friends. Don't worry if they think, *Damn, the new guy's tight.* You'll disabuse them of that notion—and divest them of their chips—before the night is through.

Bet-After-Declare Beware. If your home game is one that has a bet after the declare, you'll want to make some adjustments to maximize the opportunity and minimize the risk that this convention presents. In a typical bet-declare-bet structure, not only is there a bet after the declare, it's often the largest bet—sometimes double the size of the pre-declare round. It's not unusual, for instance, to find seven-stud HLCD with a $5–10–20 structure, where the limit is $5 through fourth street; $10 on fifth, sixth, and seventh street; and $20 after the declare. That $20 bet packs a mighty punch. It creates some opportunities to bluff—and some opportunities to get badly, badly reamed. Just think about it: If the hand has played out bet-and-call throughout all the betting streets, you will have invested $40 to get to the declare. A bet and a raise after the declare put as much money in on the last betting round as on all the prior rounds combined.

Who's going to make those bets and raises? Anyone with a lock low or a lock high, that's for sure. A single bettor going low just

loves the bet-after-declare when he's facing two or more opponents going high. The more money he can get into the pot, the
more he wins, with no risk whatsoever.

You don't want to be on the other end of that.

You sure don't want to be in a situation where the lock low
bets and a competitor for high raises. Is he bluffing? Driving a
hand worse than yours? It'll cost you another raise and a reraise to
find out. And for every dollar you bet, you stand to win only 50
cents, because the other half of the pot is spoken for. You're betting more to win less at a time when the stakes are inordinately
high. A wrong guess in this situation can easily turn a winning
night into a losing one.

How do you avoid this bad mojo? Simple. *Don't get involved.* If
the hand is shaping up to put you on the wrong end of the lock
and you're not sure you have the best holding, just dump it, while
your investment's still small. You'll more than make your money
back in other hands when you're on the right end of the lock—or
when you have a monster holding that can defeat all comers.

The presence or absence of a bet after the declare will absolutely inform your approach to the hand at hand. If there's no
bet after the declare, you can afford to speculate and you can afford to be wrong. If there is a bet after the declare, especially a
double one, you'll be punished for letting yourself get involved in
unfavorable circumstances. *Fold. Fold early, fold often.* It's just not
worth the fight.

At the same time, if you know you'll have a couple of cus-
tomers for high, say, and there's a reasonable chance that you can
grab the low for yourself, you should push hard in your isolation
attempts. Encounter legitimate resistance and you can always
back off, but the times you find yourself alone with half the pot in

a bet-declare-bet scenario will amply compensate for your isolation drives that fail.

How to Roll Your Own. In anaconda, and other roll-your-own games, you need to consider the order in which you wish your cards to appear. One rookie mistake you'll want to avoid is that of revealing the limitations of your hand too soon. Suppose you're going for low in anaconda, and you hold 2-3-4-5-8. You'll want to arrange your cards for play in this order: 5-4-3-2-8. As your opponents see your hand unfold, they can't discount the possibility that you have a wheel. They may decide to call you down, but they'll be less confident about betting into you. If your first reveal were the eight, you couldn't possibly have better than an eight low, and this would have the effect of emboldening better lows and bluffers alike.

Likewise, if you have a big full house like Q-Q-Q-5-5, hide your true strength by revealing your cards thus: 5-5-Q-Q-Q. When you turn over that first five, your foes won't know whether you're going high or low. The second five reveals that you're going high, but whether you have "fives full of something" or "something full of fives" yet remains to be seen. Even after your two queens have hit the board, it's not clear whether you have a fives boat or a queens boat, or even just two pair, and hands like 8-8-9-9-9 or J-J-J-6-6 will pay a high price to guess wrong here.

It's for just this reason that we avoid anaconda hands like low full houses and straights and flushes. Not only are they vulnerable to big full houses (an easily attainable holding in games like this), it's impossible to conceal their (lack of) strength. If you turn over 5-5-6-6, it doesn't matter whether your last card is a 6 or a 5, you have a low full house at best. If you turn over A♠-Q♠-T♠-8♠, all you can have is an ace-high flush. Anyone with as little as a weak full house knows he has you beat, and even someone bluffing with two big pair can make a decent effort to drive you off your hand.

Smart anaconda players won't even play straights, flushes, trips, or two pair, except as a shot at an isolation steal, which they'll immediately get away from in the face of any competition for the high. Similarly, they don't play mediocre lows, even if they know that the guy representing a monster low is a lying sack of cheese. Why waste chips trying to snap off bluffs in a game that offers such ample opportunity for playing with a clear lock? In other words, in anaconda and indeed throughout poker:

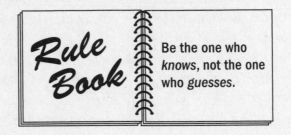

Rule Book

Be the one who *knows*, not the one who *guesses*.

Anaconda and other pass-and-roll games really reward the attentive player because there's just a *ton* of quality information to draw upon.

The guy to my right passed me a deuce and a trey? Well, he's sure as hell not going low. Sure enough, he turns over a jack and then a jack, and since I'm showing a pair of queens, it looks like he's going to bash himself against the remorseless walls of my big full house. But, oops, his next reveal is an ace. Could he have aces full of jacks? No, his fourth card is a jack. Now he's showing J-J-A-J, and he can't beat a queens boat!

But hang on. I know this guy. He never reveals his full strength before he has to. If he had either jacks full of aces or aces full of jacks, I'd be looking at J-J-A-A right now. He's only got three of a kind. He's dead meat!

Or is he? Think, John, *have you ever seen this guy go four cards deep into anaconda with a hand as weak as trips? No. Never. Not if there's competition for the high.*

Looks like he's sitting on four jacks.

Wowee.

Good thing I've got four queens.

Manipulating Position. Various games give you different opportunities to exploit, or be exploited by, position. Let's take a quick look at some of them now.

In roll-your-own games, the high card or high hand leads the betting. If you have a low hand containing an ace, don't put the ace up first, even though it's a strong card, for you'll have to bet first on every round of betting until a pair pops up. Should you then find yourself up against a solid low or a solid low bluff, you may have to check, indicating weakness, and then call raises and reraises that you might not be too thrilled to call. If you put your deuce in the door, at least some people will have to act before you do, plus you won't have revealed any vital information about your hand (like the fact that you have an ace).

In draw poker, lowball, and community card games like hold'em and Omaha, it's typical for the person to the left of the blinds to act first—but not every home game plays with a blind. If you're not obligated to open the betting, I strongly recommend that you check, no matter what the strength of your hand. That way, when someone behind you bets, you're suddenly "in position," last to act, or late to act, after everyone between you and the bettor has already told you how they feel about their hand.

This move is powerful whether or not check-raising is allowed in your game. If check-raising is allowed, you've kept your options open, and can reraise the original bettor if circumstances deem. Where check-raising is not allowed, you know that no one who has checked behind you can raise you now. This allows you to make some calls you otherwise would not be able to make if you feared additional raises from players downstream.

In later betting rounds in these draw or flop games, it's standard practice for the player to the left of the dealer to open the action, but again, not every poker night plays it this way. In some games, the person who took the last bet or raise on the previous betting round is first to act on the next. This devalues the strength of your raise, for if you take the last bet on the flop, say, you have to act first on the turn, letting everyone behind you know where you stand on the hand. In a game that follows this betting convention, you sometimes have to raise anyhow, because the strength of your hand demands it. If someone reraises you, though, just call instead of raising him back. That way, you've built reasonable volume in the pot, but he has to start the next round of betting and you can benefit from any information he gives away.

In games like five-card stud and seven-card stud, where the best hand leads the action, it's always a good idea to keep your eye on where that best hand is. If there's *a pair in the air* (an open pair onboard), that pair is going to be leading the betting for a while. If it's on your left, you have good relative position and some flexibility in your action. If it's on your right, you'll have to act early, with all the hazards that implies. A hand that's playable with strength on your left might be a clear fold with strength on your right.

Most players won't give a second thought to questions of position. They never look past their own hands and their imperfect appraisal of whether it will hold up for a win. If you pay attention to position, you'll make the most of favorable situations and avoid trouble that others might not even see. You'll be cleverer than them, but don't alert them to that fact, for they might just go ahead and change the game conditions to neutralize whatever advantage you've managed to find. On the other hand, don't worry too much if they do, for there's positional advantage to be had, no matter what the game or betting protocol. Seize it where you can, and you give yourself that much more edge over those who don't.

Watching the Watchers. Much is made in popular culture of the so-called *poker face*, the deadpan countenance that hides a poker player's, or anyone's, true intent. For my money, no one has ever matched Clint Eastwood's Man with No Name, with his thousand-yard stare and that cheroot manfully jammed in the corner of his mouth. Anyone who has ever picked up a poker hand, though, imagines himself to be a master of the mask, one who gives nothing away.

In fact, most poker players are not nearly as impassive as they'd like to believe, especially home game players who have occasion to unpack their poker faces only once a week or once a month. They may think they're being fairly clever by screwing their brows down when they're bluffing or smiling broadly when they want you to call, but these are unpracticed deceptions, codes easily cracked. They'd be just as well served to turn their faces to the wall and let you try and guess from their asses what they have. Still, anyone with his guard up can do a half-decent job of blunt-

ing his reactions, so the trick is to watch your foes when their
guard is down. Just wait for those moments when people aren't
expecting you to be looking at them, then make it a point to look.

A classic case is the flop in hold'em. When that flop comes
down, it's natural for everyone to direct their attention *right there*.
Why not? That's where their future sorrow or happiness lies,
right? Well, the flop will still be there in another five seconds—
you can look later—but your foes' unguarded reactions to it will
be gone. So while everyone is looking at the flop, you look at them.
They may give nothing away, but then again they might. A twitch
of the mouth, a slump of the shoulders, a puff of the cheeks . . .
any of these things could tell you how they feel about the cards
they've just seen.

If they're very tricky, they might lie, assuming they know
you're looking, but that would mean that they're both tricky *and*
observant, a rare enough breed in most home games. You, being
both tricky and observant, will of course know if you're studying
someone with good skills in deception, in which case you can discount or ignore the information you receive, or else just direct
your efforts at someone who's easier to read.

Wherever your attention goes, it should *not* go to the cards.
Watch the players when they watch the flop. Watch them when
they look at their replacements in draw or lowball, or the cards
they get dealt in stud or passed in anaconda. When you *look at the
players instead of the cards*, three good things can happen. First, as
we've already discussed, you might gather some useful information; you might pick off a real tell. Second, you minimize the risk
of your own reaction giving anything away. After all, there's no
guarantee that you yourself have perfected Clint's thousand-yard
stare, but no one can know how you like a card if you haven't
bothered to look yet. Third, you bring your thinking about poker

to a higher level. If you're the only one at the table who bothers to study others' reactions to the turn of certain cards, you're probably better than them in other ways as well.

And that's really the goal, you know: to bring your thinking to a higher level. Whether you're satisfied to dominate poker night or you're looking to move from home games to cardroom poker, your growth requires that you find ever more detailed and articulate ways to think about the game you play. No one masters poker overnight, but everyone can grow in their skills and understanding, if they just commit themselves to walking down that road.

♦ ♦ ♦ FAQs

Here are some frequently asked questions about home poker that get, you know, frequently asked.

How should I handle running out of cards in the middle of the hand?

It's awkward, to say the least, to run out of cards during the deal. With some games, like six gun or five-card Omaha (big O), you simply don't deal the game if you have more players than the deck can handle: six players in six gun and eight in big O. With other games, like seven-card stud and its variations, you should theoretically not be able to deal to more than seven players because that's the maximum number of complete hands you can get out of a 52-card deck. In practice, though, someone usually folds, so in home games and even in cardrooms people feel comfortable dealing seven-stud eight-handed (though usually not more).

Still, it can happen that there aren't enough cards to go around, so you'll need a procedure to cover that circumstance. Here's the simplest one I know. If the dealer determines that there aren't enough cards left in the deck for everyone to get a "fresh" one, he simply burns the top card, then turns over the next card as a common card for everyone left in the hand. In some games, it's the practice to shuffle all discards and give everyone a new card from that stack. That works, too, but many players feel that folded cards are "tainted" somehow. The common card method assures, at minimum, a patently level playing field.

Whether you shuffle the discards or use a common card, it's wise to announce your policy before the hand begins or to include it in your house rules. That way, there will be no arguments or hard feelings, and anyone feeling constrained to complain can be directed to the NO WHINGING rule.

What does it mean to "burn and turn"?

Burning and turning is a dealing protocol that protects the top card of the deck from being exposed accidentally by a clumsy dealer or manipulated adventitiously by a crooked one. Instead of dealing the top card in the deck, the dealer "burns" that card by placing it facedown in front of him, then commences the deal with the next card in sequence.

Burn and turn is standard practice in all cardrooms. You don't see it quite so much in home games, but there's no reason not to make it a part of yours. It looks nice, it regulates dealing procedure, and it instills a certain sense of security. Something about "Caesar's wife must be above suspicion" comes to mind here, though I must tell you that while burning the top card will minimize the impact of maladroit dealing, it won't do much to stop a scalawag who's determined to deal seconds or otherwise *futz* (stack) the deck to his own benefit.

What should I do if I find a cheater in my game?
String him up by his thumbs.

Seriously, let's talk about cheating for a second. Let me start with these reassuring words: In most home games, players who resort to cheating are so monumentally bad to begin with that they can't beat the game, even by outlaw methods. Nevertheless, there's no place in home games for cheaters. They're depressing and they cause bad blood.

There are two different classes of cheating, what we might call active cheating and passive cheating. An active cheater might commit any or all of these sins:

- *Shorting the pot.* To short the pot means to toss in your chips in such a way that no one can tell whether you made a full bet or not. To prevent this infraction (or even honest confusion), ask players not to *splash the pot* with their chips and instead have each player put his bets directly in front of him, pushing them into the pot only after the betting round is complete and everyone has fully met all bets and raises.
- *Peeking.* Scoundrels can peek either by looking at the cards as they deal them or, you know, leaning over to see what the other guy has. The latter is pretty blatant—and therefore rare. If you suspect someone of the former, just watch his eyes to see if he's inordinately focused on the deck as he deals.
- *Futzing the deck.* Any time someone deliberately arranges or deals the cards in such a way as to give himself an advantage, he's committing a crime against nature—or anyway against the nature of poker night. Good procedures for shuffling and cutting the cards, plus burning and turning will take this weapon out of his hand. A watchful eye never hurts, either.
- *Misdeclaring a hand.* A determined angle shooter might de-

clare that he has a big hand in hopes that the other players will muck their cards and he can collect the pot sight unseen. It's venal and nasty, but easily stopped. Just play *cards speak* and never surrender your hand until the evidence of your eyes tell you it's beaten.

- *Marking cards.* A crease here, a crimp there, and soon a crumb knows the location of every ace in the deck. The bad news is, many home game decks aren't all that pristine to begin with, and even if they start the night off new, they get worked around pretty good by honest, albeit ham-handed, players. The good news is, most home game cheats aren't deft enough to pull this off. Best protection: two fresh, sealed decks of cards every time you play, plus the aforementioned watchful eye.

- *Stalling or balking.* Angle shooters will delay their bets or declares in hopes of gaining information that will allow them to alter or amend their own playing decisions. As we've already discussed, information of this sort is not necessarily ill-gotten; it may have been gleaned from tells. To neutralize legitimate and illegitimate edges alike, just take all your actions carefully and never do anything until it's your turn to act.

- *Collusion.* Two or more cheaters in the same game can collude in a number of ways: by sharing coded information about the cards they hold; by agreeing in advance to treat each other favorably in card-passing games; by surreptitiously exchanging cards; by *whipsawing* other players (raising and reraising one another in hopes of trapping an unsuspecting third party for many bets). If you've got two or more cheaters in your game, get a new game.

- *Palming chips.* A creep making change from the pot or splitting the pot at the end of the hand has the opportunity to extract a little extra value by palming a chip or two. You can't imagine that someone would do this for 25 or 50 cents, but you'd be amazed at how low some people can sink. Solutions include letting only the bank make change and letting only the winners split the pot. A more easygoing alternative is just to play with people you can trust.

If you catch an active cheater, just bar him—Ross his raggedy ass. Allowing a cheat, even a loser (even a big loser), at your table will degrade the spirit of the game and defeat the very purpose of poker night.

Passive cheaters are not so much blackguards as opportunists. They won't crane their heads to look at your cards, for example, but they won't go out of their way not to look, either. With this we get into an ethical gray area, because each player does have the responsibility to protect his own cards from prying eyes, and no player has a moral obligation not to see what's right in front of his face. Home game procedures can get quite sloppy, and extra information is often on offer for those who are naturally attentive to begin with.

Moral relativism is a slippery slope. You won't short the pot, but will you tell another player if he puts in too much? You won't misdeclare your hand, but what if they push you a pot that's not rightfully yours? You won't peek at the bottom card while you shuffle or cut (though some would), but what if the dealer exposes that card while he deals? Here's a thought: When in doubt, always act in a manner that is beyond reproach. That way you're Caesar's wife in perception *and* in fact. And if it costs you an extra chip or two along the way, well, you'll get your reward in heaven.

I must tell you, though, in the thousands of poker nights I've been to, I've never seen any significant instances of cheating, either active or passive. You could argue, I suppose, that they're too clever for me and they just didn't get caught. Maybe, but I'd rather consider a game honest until proven crooked. That way I can concentrate on playing my best without getting all paranoid and weird.

What should I do about "stressors," people who get cranky when they lose?

Some folks are simply poor sports. That's just a fact of life. I've seen people lose $20, $10, even pretend money, and go completely insane over the loss. You'd think their world had come to an end, and you'd think that, seeing themselves go through this hell, they'd avoid playing poker ever again in life. Yet they're the first ones with the follow-up phone call saying, "When's the next poker night?" And they're the first to go insane again when they lose.

What to do about these *stressors*? You can't lose to them on purpose, or even ease up on them, just to save them from their own suffering. It wouldn't be fair to the rest of the players to yield to this form of emotional blackmail. You may find it hard to give them the boot, especially if they're close friends of yours or of other poker night regulars. You could, I suppose, slip them a Xanax, but . . . nah, probably a bad idea.

Being a conflict-avoider from way back, I'd probably try to raise the issue without putting myself in the middle of a big confrontation. In other words, I'd lie. "Look," I'd say, "I'm not naming names, but you're making some of the other players uncomfortable. We all lose from time to time, and we try to take it in stride. If you can't do that, maybe you'd better look for another game."

Seriously, a healthy poker game is a thing to be tended and

nurtured. In a very real sense, the good of the game comes ahead of individual needs. Players who don't contribute to that greater good must necessarily find themselves on the outside looking in.

How should *I* cope with losing?

Losing is part of winning. If you hit the target every time, the target is either too big or too close. Every poker player experiences losing sessions, and professionals can go through slumps that literally last years. Mental toughness is called for here, and a clear understanding of the difference between *review* and *regret*.

When things go wrong, review your play with an eye toward improving it. If, at the end of review, you can conclude that you did everything right but just got unlucky, then trust that luck will even out in the end. If you made mistakes, acknowledge those mistakes and figure out how to avoid repeating them. This proactive stance, this *I'll do better next time* attitude, will go a long way toward taking off the sting off a loss.

Meanwhile, don't get caught in regret, for if you carry regret forward from the past into the future it can only continue to poison your state of mind and reinfect your play. Whether it's a hand that went wrong thirty seconds ago, or last night's game that was a freaking disaster, or a whole past month or year that you've been running bad, you have to let it go. Study. Learn. Review. Take note, then *move on*. The past is past. It can't touch you anymore. I don't suppose it will help much to say that "What doesn't kill you makes you stronger," but it's true. Every setback you suffer makes you tougher if you let it.

How do I shuffle chips?

Place two equal stacks of chips beside each other on the table. Put your thumb on the left side of the two stacks and your second and third fingers on the right (reverse if left-handed). Using your index finger to lift the stacks in the middle where they touch, gently push toward the center with your thumb and fingers. This should give you a nice, smooth, interleaving chip riffle. *Hint:* Start with six, get good at shuffling two stacks of three chips each, and then move up as your dexterity improves.

Don't be intimidated by a player who can shuffle his chips, or finger roll them, or balance them on the tip of his nose. Yes, he's been handling chips long enough to become an expert—but maybe only expert at handling chips! He might be a strong player, or he might just be spending *way* too much time at the table.

Focus your attention on how they *play*, not on how they "play."

What's the Dead Man's Hand?

Two pair, aces and eights, is the hand Wild Bill Hickok was holding when Jack McCall plugged him in the back (and taught us all not to sit with our backs to the door). While there's no reason you can't give cards or hands your own names—I've always called K♣-Q♣ *Big Maxx*, just 'cause I thought my wife should have a hand named after her—here's a short list of other nicknames or handles you can drop into card table conversation to make yourself sound like a wise guy or, at minimum, a wiseguy.

T-4 has long been known as *Broderick Crawford*, thanks to his signature signoff.

Aces are *bullets* because that's what they look like.

Pocket eights are commonly called *dog balls* (turn them sideways to see), though I prefer *double infinity*.

A-K-4-7 in Omaha is an *assault rifle*.

3-3-3 is a *forest* (tree-tree-tree).

6-9 has many innuendo interpretations, including the least indelicate, *dinner for two*.

9-5 is *Dolly Parton*, because of that movie she was in, but 3-8 is *Raquel Welch* and 2-9 is *Twiggy* for more directly anatomical reasons.

K-9 is a *mongrel*, but K-9 suited is a *pedigree*.

2-4 is the *lumberman's hand* (two-by-four, get it?)

Two queens are *mopsqueezers* or *Sigfried and Roy* or any number of other politically incorrect assignations; Q-3 is a *gay waiter*, queen with a trey.

9-9 is a *German virgin* because *"Nein, nein"* is all she ever says.

T-7 is a *split*, borrowed from bowling.

7-2 is a *beer hand*, presumably because you have time to go get one after you fold.

A *Doyle Brunson* is T-2, the final hand he held in back-to-back World Series of Poker wins.

Should I teach my children to play poker?

By all means. Your children. Nieces and nephews. Kids down the block. To endow a young person with a clear understanding of poker is to do that child a great service. Beyond the obvious instruction in basic math, probability, and money management, poker teaches psychology and human nature and gives us deep insight into our own nature. It tests us in a certain crucible. It tempers us.

Poker is a survival skill. Just ask Richard Nixon, who funded his first congressional race with poker winnings racked up during a stint in the South Seas. Or ask any of my nieces or nephews whose expertise at hold'em kept them in CDs and sub sandwiches throughout their college years.

Poker is a social skill. If you know how to play the game, you can sit down at a table with strangers and walk away friends. Deals are negotiated over poker games. Strategic alliances struck. Careers advanced.

More than anything, poker builds character. It teaches us how to win with grace and how to lose with dignity. It teaches us how to get along with people of wildly different temperaments and backgrounds. It teaches us how to keep our head when all around us are losing theirs.

Am I concerned about raising a generation of degenerate gamblers? To the contrary. A young person who knows what it means to bet with the best of it is far less likely to throw away his money on no-win propositions like keno or carny games. Poker players, schooled in odds and steeled by outcomes, have a healthy disdain for that which seems too good to be true. Per Damon Runyon:

> "Son," a father tells his boy, "no matter how far you travel in this world or how smart you get, always remember this. Someday, somewhere, a guy is going to come to you and show you a brand-new deck of cards on which the seal is never broken, and this guy is going to offer to bet you that the jack of spades will jump out of this deck and squirt cider in your ear. But son, do not bet him, for as sure as you do, you are going to get an earful of cider."

A poker player would know better. If you have kids, it's never too soon to clue them in.

17

BEER MONEY AND BRAGGING RIGHTS

♠

Always an egalitarian game to begin with, poker has truly been given to the masses in recent years. What was a broadly, though quietly, popular game across a swath of American society has now become as much a part of our cultural landscape as hit movies, pop music, or the latest superstar scandal. People who had never even seen a poker game two years ago can now recount (and second-guess!) the final table exploits of Phil Hellmuth, Annie Duke, and other favorites of the World Poker Tour. Modern anthropologists call this the *water cooler phenomenon*: When something becomes so well known as to be the subject of conversation around workplace water coolers, it has arrived.

Two technological advancements have driven poker's sudden surge into the mainstream. The first was the advent of internet poker, which has allowed anyone with even a passing interest in the game to get all the play they can handle, no matter where they happen to be. Now no longer limited to Las Vegas, Atlantic City, and other outposts and oases, poker—serious poker—can take root and grow in every house on the block.

Then came the lipstick cam. This tiny technology, a video camera the size of a lipstick tube, made it possible to show the players' hole cards in televised poker tournaments, turning an event formerly as interesting as watching paint dry into something truly spellbinding. Now the folks at home can watch the pros set traps, press edges, run massive bluffs, and step on land mines. The thrill of this is not unlike the visceral kick you get from watching movie heroes approaching the monster's lair. You know the danger lurks; they don't. It's made all the difference in the world, expanding televised poker from ESPN's once-a-year coverage of the World Series of Poker to weekly broadcasts of World Poker Tour events, plus *The Celebrity Poker Showdown*, the WPT's *Hollywood Home Game*, *Late Night Poker from Great Britain*, and who knows what's coming next. The legitimization of poker became complete on February 1, 2004, when NBC broadcast a World Poker Tour contest as counterprogramming to the Super Bowl pregame show.

With all of America watching over the pros' shoulders and playing along on their computers, poker now enjoys a level of popularity and social acceptance that would make the old-time Texas rounders take off their ten-gallon hats and rub their scalps in wonder. It has come charging out of smoky back rooms and sordid speakeasies smack-dab into the public eye. No wonder so many people who'd never given poker the time of day now suddenly can't wait to play.

Which brings us back to this book, at the end of which we both now stand. I hope and trust that you've gotten sufficient value for the time and the money you invested in it. If all has gone according to plan, you now have new, or renewed, enthusiasm for poker night, plus all the information you need to set up and run a game—and the knowledge and confidence to win beer money and bragging rights from your friends. You also have a ready reference for when disputes arise about how to go light, who gets the odd chip in a split pot, or what's a perfect low. I don't imagine that this book will become the Hoyle of home poker, but I wouldn't mind knowing that your copy got a little dog-eared over time.

"You can't enter the same river twice," says the sage, because when you next visit it, both you and the river will have changed. I hope you'll have occasion to revisit this book later in your poker education and evolution. I think you'll find that some of the material hits you differently then. Maybe some things that weren't clear the first time through will be more accessible on the second pass. Maybe your subsequent experience of poker will have rendered everything herein old hat. Maybe your own explorations and discoveries will lead you to look back on some of my ideas and say, "Man, is that guy out to lunch." You wouldn't be the first.

Your poker journey can take you many places: into cardrooms; onto the internet; out on the tournament trail; to a seat in front of a lipstick cam . . . or just from one poker night to the next. Wherever you play, the most important thing you can do is be honest with yourself. Make sure you're making that raise because it's the strategically correct thing to do and not just because you're cheesed off at the guy who bet into you. Make sure you're calling a bet because the odds warrant it, not because you just can't bear to fold and be out of action. Above all, make sure you're playing poker because you *want* to, not because you have to. Poker is compelling; I find it addictive in a good way, but when it shifts from hobby to habit or obsession, then the fun stops, and I'd hate to see that happen to you. Keep poker night in its proper place: a healthy part of a balanced, thoughtful life.

If you have read this book and your poker night companions

have not, there's a good chance that you will quickly become much better than they are. Be *very quiet* about this fact. They don't need to know how good you are, and if you insist on telling them, you run the risk of making them play better against you— and making it harder for you to take their money next time. Given a choice between feeding your ego or padding your bankroll, opt for the bankroll every time. In other words, though this book may earn you bragging rights, you might have to keep your bragging to yourself.

In another context, I once wrote about something called my whole-life résumé, not a list of jobs I've held but of things I've done that make me feel like my years on this planet have been well spent. Winning an Ultimate Frisbee world championship. Marrying a woman I love. Seeing my books in bookstores.

Playing poker.

Getting together with good friends, sharing food and drink, exchanging laughs and lies.

Then pummeling them senseless in the game.

Home poker has been a cherished part of my life. I hope it becomes a cherished part of yours, too. And now if you'll excuse me, I have to go. Tonight is poker night, and I sure don't want to be late.

GLOSSARY

♠

Part of the pleasure of poker is its language. When you can deftly describe yourself as an *Omaholic flophead* who hit *runner-runner* and turned some real *cheese* into the *nuts* for a big *suckout* and a monster *scoop*, you kind of feel like you've arrived. Below you'll find some words from this book. Most are common poker slang, but some are words I coined or encountered in home games here and there. And remember: Just as you're free to invent deviant poker games, you're also free to invent your own poker slang. "When I use a word," said Humpty Dumpty, "it means just what I choose it to mean—neither more nor less."

Active sonar: a raise intended to gather information about the strength of an opponent's hand
Backpredict: retrospective analysis of the play of a hand
Bad beat: losing a pot with a hand that's a heavy favorite to win
Bank: the person responsible for cashing the players in and out of the game

Big Bens or Franklins: $100 bills

Blinds: forced bets designed to start the action

Brick: an unhelpful card

Bring-in: a forced bet in stud-style games

Bug: the joker, used in lowball and other poker variations

Buy-in: the initial amount of money needed to get into the game

Case card: a single card left in the deck that can help or complete one's hand

Check: decline to bet, while reserving the right to call or raise later

Cheese: scandalously bad cards

Clean out: a card that improves only one player's hand and no others

Dangler: a disconnected fourth card in an Omaha hand

Dealer's choice: a home poker convention where the dealer selects the game to be played

Door card: the first exposed card in five-card or seven-card stud

Downstream: players yet to act after you

Eight must or qualified low: high-low poker where the low hand must contain five different cards ranked eight or below

Flop: the first three community cards in hold'em or Omaha

Flophead: someone committed to seeing every *flop*

Free roll: drawing to improve one's hand while already holding the best hand, or drawing for the high or low half of the pot while already holding a lock in the other direction

Futz: to tamper with or stack the deck

Gamnesia: the tendency of a gambler to forget how much he lost

Ghost: to observe another player or players when you're not in the hand

Go light: to borrow money from the pot until the conclusion of the hand

Go pig: to declare both high and low in a high-low chip declare game

Grab: an easily remembered and understood poker tip

Gulp limit: the *buy-in* amount where players start to get nervous

HLCD: high-low, chip-declare

Hole cards: a player's hidden cards in flop- or stud-style games

In boss command: ahead in the hand

Kicker: the side card to a pair or two pair

Limits: the smallest and largest size bets allowed in a poker game

Lock: guaranteed win

Make up one's lights: repay the money borrowed from the pot in the process of going light

Nut high: the best possible high hand

Nut low: the best possible low hand

Nuts: an unbeatable hand

Omaholic: a devotee of Omaha/8

On the bubble: one place away from a money-winning finish in a poker tournament

Outs: cards that will "get you out on top," i.e., give you a winning hand

Paint: a picture card

Packet: a working two-card combination in Omaha or Omaha/8

Pot odds: the projected return on investment for a given bet, measured against the chances of making one's hand

Quarter: to split half of half a pot, and possibly lose money on the hand

Rack off: to lose all your money (every chip in your rack)

Rags: a ragged hand; lousy cards

Rainbow: unsuited

Raisitis: a mental affliction that makes a player raise all the time

Rake: the money collected by the house as a fee for hosting the game

Ring game: a cash game as opposed to a poker tournament

River: the fifth and final community card in hold'em or Omaha

Rossed: banned from the game

Rough low: a low-quality low hand, for instance 8-7-6-3-2, a *rough eight*

Runner-runner: two consecutive cards needed to make your hand, as in "a runner-runner flush draw"

Scoop: to win both sides of a high-low split pot

Smooth low: a high-quality low hand, for instance 7-4-3-2-A, a *smooth seven*

Suckout: a lucky win against long odds

Swing: the amount of money that a player stands to win or lose in a typical home poker session

Table stakes: the amount of money a player has on the table when a hand begins.

Tilt or **on tilt:** playing angry, impatiently, recklessly, or otherwise out of control

Tell: an unconscious gesture that betrays the strength of your hand or your betting intention

Turn: the fourth community card in hold'em or Omaha

Twist: a replacement card purchased after the final cards are dealt

Under the gun: first to act

Weevil: to go broke quickly

Wheel or bicycle: the best hand in lowball, A-2-3-4-5

Whiff: to get cards that don't help you in any way

Whinge: to complain fretfully, or whine; an infraction punishable by death

RECOMMENDED READING

♠

Every single poker book I've read had something to offer me, even if only an opinion or a strategy I didn't understand or flat-out disagreed with. In fact, those books may be the most useful, for ideas that challenge or confound me are the ones that most stimulate my thinking—and that's where real learning takes place.

If this book has given you a thirst for more poker knowledge, there's no shortage of places you can go to slake that thirst. Most major bookstores these days have healthy sections on poker strategy for players at every level of development, and if you go into a specialty store like the Gambler's Book Shop or the Gamblers General Store in Las Vegas, the number of poker titles on offer will quickly boggle your mind. A few key books and authors have really helped me grow, and I'd be shocked if they didn't help you, too.

- Doyle Brunson's *Super/System: A Course in Power Poker* is the grand-daddy of all poker books, and while some of its content has been overtaken by events, it's still required reading for any serious poker practitioner.

- Mike Caro, "America's Mad Genius of Poker," has written numerous industry-standard poker books, including *Caro's Fundamental Secrets of Poker* and *Mike Caro's Book of Poker Tells*. Not to put too fine a point on it, if Caro says it, it must be true.

- John Fox's *Play Poker, Quit Work and Sleep Till Noon* is one of my all-time favorites. Its focus on draw poker makes it outdated in today's frenzy of flop games, but the underlying concepts are still sound and his timeless writing style is refreshingly avaricious.

- If you're up to the challenge, Phil Hellmuth's *Play Poker Like the Pros* will give you sophisticated moves and countermoves for almost any hold'em situation you can name.

- Both Lee Jones's *Winning Low Limit Hold'em* and Lou Krieger's *Hold'em Excellence: From Beginner to Winner* are indispensable introductions to entry-level cardroom hold'em; don't leave home without 'em.

- The *Championship* series by top tournament pros Tom McEvoy and T. J. Cloutier will give you everything you need to know about poker tournament strategy and tactics.

- *Championship Satellite Strategy* by Tom McEvoy and Brad Daughterty deconstructs the specialized world of tournament satellites, an increasingly popular and important area of poker interest.

- George Percy's *7-Card Stud: The Waiting Game* remains the best basic stud guide there is.

- David Sklansky's *Theory of Poker* is the last word in poker mathematics. If numbers are your thing, anything by Sklansky or his partner, Mason Malmuth, will be your cup of tea.

- I suppose I'd be remiss, or anyway missing a shot at shameless self-promotion, if I didn't mention my own *Killer Poker* series of books: *Killer Poker: Strategy and Tactics for Winning Poker Play; Killer Poker Online: Crushing the Internet Game;* and *The Killer Poker Hold'em Handbook: A Workbook for Winners.* If you like what you've read here, you'll find more of the same there.

Books, of course, are not the only source of poker information available to you. The internet is rife with poker strategy sites, poker discussion groups, and online poker portals. Any extensive list of such resources would naturally become outdated over time, so rather than risk pointing you to a disappointing *404: File Not Found,* I'll recommend a few sites that seem to be here to stay. You can use these as points of departure to a wider, indeed virtually endless, exploration of poker on the web.

- www.cardplayer.com is the online version of the venerable poker magazine *Card Player*. Here you will find rankings of the game's top players, tips of the week, and even a handy point-and-click odds calculator.

- If odds are your thing, check out the Mike Caro Poker University at www.caro.com, which features many statistical tables, plus archived lectures, quizzes, and other learning tools.

- www.pokerpages.com offers a worldwide cardroom directory and a complete schedule of daily, weekly, and annual poker tournaments. This is also the jumping-off point to Poker School Online, where you can continue your poker education in a community of like-minded souls.

- www.twoplustwo.com is the online home of poker theorists and math wonks David Sklansky and Mason Malmuth. Their 2+2 Forums host some of the net's most erudite poker discussion and analysis.

- Through www.groups.google.com you can reach rec.gambling.poker, the long-running (and sometimes raucous) unmoderated discussion group of all things poker. RGPers, as you'll discover, are some of the game's most outspoken and colorful characters.

- At my own website, www.vorza.com, you'll find an archive of my poker writings, plus nonpoker writings, nonsense, non sequiturs, and an easy means of ordering my (autographed) books online.

INDEX

♠

ABOUT THE AUTHOR

♠

John Vorhaus has written more than two million words about poker. When not writing about poker or playing poker, he writes screenplays and television shows, and travels internationally teaching others how to do these things. His seminal writing books, *The Comic Toolbox* and *Creativity Rules!*, have guided and informed writers worldwide, and his *Killer Poker* series of books has likewise inspired countless poker players to "go big or go home." He lives in Monrovia, California, with his wife, Maxx Duffy, and his dogs, Dodger and Ranger, and abides in cyberspace at www.vorza.com.